TWILIGHT OF
SOUTH AFRICAN STEAM

*A pair of class 25NC teams up to hurry a northbound
freight from Bloemfontein to Bethlehem, and are seen
climbing the gradient approaching Ionia siding.*

TWILIGHT OF
SOUTH AFRICAN
STEAM

A E Durrant

DAVID & CHARLES
Newton Abbot · London

(title page) *Reflected in the floodwaters in the middle of the 1983 drought (!) a class GMAM Garratt heads north towards Mafeking with a freight from Vryburg.*

Abbreviations used

Alco	American Locomotive Company
Cape E.	Cape Eastern Region
Cape M.	Cape Midland Region
Cape N.	Cape Northern Region
Cape W.	Cape Western Region
CFM	Caminhos de Ferro Moçambique (Moçambique Railways)
CGR	Cape Government Railway
CME	Chief Mechanical Engineer
CSAR	Central South African Railways
DR	Deutches Reichsbahn
E. Tvl	Eastern Transvaal
GWR	Great Western Railway (of Great Britain)
NGR	Natal Government Railways
NRZ	National Railways of Zimbabwe
NZASM	Nederlandsche Zuid Afrikaansche Spoorweg Maatschappij (Dutch South African Railway Company)
OFS	Orange Free State
RR	Rhodesia Railways
RSSA	Railway Society of Southern Africa
SA	South Africa
SAR	South African Railways
SAR&H	South African Railways and Harbours
SATS	South African Transport Services
SNCZ	Societe Nationale des Chemins de Fer Zairois (Zaire Railways)
SR	Swaziland Railways

All photographs by the author unless otherwise credited

British Library Cataloguing in Publication Data

Durrant, A. E. (Anthony Edward) *1929–*
    Twilight of South African steam.
    1. South Africa. Steam locomotives, history
    I. Title
    625.2′61′0968

ISBN 0-7153-8638-7

Typeset by Typesetters (Birmingham) Limited,
Smethwick, West Midlands
and printed in Great Britain
by Redwood Burn Limited,
Trowbridge, Wilts
for David & Charles Publishers plc
Brunel House   Newton Abbot   Devon

Contents

Main line 1985! A pair of class 25NC blast out of Orange River early on a February morning in 1985. The southbound train was the fourth seen between dawn and 08.30, while most people were having a Sunday 'lie-in'.

Introduction

Until 1970, comparatively little had been written about the steam locomotives of South Africa, other than technical descriptions of new locomotives as built, the major coherent account being by Espitalier and Day in the pages of the SAR&H magazine. Then in 1972 came two major works, the two-part complete history of 3ft 6in gauge SAR locomotives, by D. F. Holland (published by David & Charles) and *Steam on the Veld*, co-authored by the present writer, a largely pictorial account of the country's steam in action during the late 1960s—the two works being largely complementary. These books effectively placed SAR steam locomotives on the world map, since when thousands of enthusiasts have visited South Africa solely to experience these magnificent monsters at work. Several dozen, realising that one could see only a little within the usual few weeks' visit, have settled in the country, for a better look.

As steam dwindled in South Africa, the local Railway Society of Southern Africa became more active. In particular it ran some spectacular steam specials of which the Sunset Limited in 1979 proved so successful that SAR in turn used the formula for a series of 'Steam Safaris' run and marketed mainly for overseas tourists. Arising from these, some strange claims have been made, such that South Africa is the 'last bastion of steam traction in the World'(!). Actually in 1984 South Africa came fourth in the steam stakes, behind China whose steam population was about 10,000, with steam still under construction, India with around 8,000, and Poland with perhaps 2,000 locomotives. However, of these countries, South Africa was by far the easiest one in which to travel, with good hotels, car hire, and friendly authorities which the other countries lack either wholly or in part. Added attractions for South Africa are the excellent scenery and good weather, making photography very rewarding.

Locomotive development in South Africa from the turn of the century to the 1950s had been quite spectacular, with SAR steam being on several occasions larger and more powerful than anywhere outside North America. Notwithstanding the broader gauges used elsewhere, SAR steam was particularly more advanced than in the other spheres of British influence such as India, Australia, and Argentina. Quantitatively, SAR had the largest steam stock of any individual railway in the Southern Hemisphere. Of countries having large narrow (ie less than standard 4ft 8½in or 1,435mm) gauges, South Africa at maximum came third behind Japan with around 5,000 steam locomotives mainly of 3ft 6in gauge, and India with around 4,000, the majority of metre gauge.

Bearing in mind what has previously been published, this book concentrates mainly on the period from 1973 to 1989, but does commence with a chapter briefly outlining SAR steam development from the very early days until the 1950s. The bulk of the book covers the relevant years in more detail than has been previously published, firstly with a class-by-class locomotive summary, followed by a regional survey showing locomotives at work in their latter years. During the period covered, numerous SAR locomotives were sold or hired to neighbouring countries, and these are detailed as accurately as possible, although some places were too hostile or down-right dangerous to allow visits by even the most intrepid enthusiast and his camera! Finally, during these years a large number of SAR locomotives have been sold to industry which has heeded the South African government's exhortations to conserve oil supplies, even to the extent of replacing diesels by second-hand steam locomotives. The full story of industrial steam in South Africa is too large and complex for one book, and the account within limits itself to ex-SAR locomotives sold from 1973 onwards.

The last section deals with steam development in South Africa following the 1970s oil crises. One man only on SAR was sufficiently convinced of steam's economic supremacy to force through a programme of steam development, using two guinea-pig locomotives. The results from these made management take notice to the extent of instigating an enquiry into the economic merits of the three traction forms—confidently expecting steam to come a poor third! Horror! Steam was found the most economic!

Details of these results, together with an extrapolation as to the type of steam that could be built in South Africa, bring the book to a controversial end.

A. E. Durrant
Springs, South Africa

CHAPTER 1

South African Locomotive Development

South African Railways was formed in 1910 from three major constituents, the Cape Government Railway, Natal Government Railway and the Central South African Railways, each of which had developed its own designs for what was the common task of bringing heavy loads from the coast to the interior, characterised by the *Highveld*, or central plateau, roughly a mile above sea level. Successful designs needed high tractive effort allied to reliable adhesion, high steaming capacities, and the ability to negotiate sharp curves. The use of relatively heavy rail at any given period meant that SAR locomotives, despite their narrow gauge of 3ft 6in (1,067mm, today rounded-off as 1,065mm) have usually been exceeded in power only by the giants of North America, with standard and broad gauge locomotives in other parts of the world being generally less powerful than SAR equivalents, other than odd classes built in small quantities. Bearing the above in mind, we may now look at the main constituent railways, their basic lines of development, and how much or how little they affected post-Union practice.

Central South African Railways

Although a major constituent, the effect of this organisation on later SAR development was zero. Itself composed of various subsidiary railways amalgamated in 1902, the majority of its motive power was inherited from the Nederlandsche Zuid Afrikaansche Spoorweg Maatschappij, the line backed by President Kruger, and routed from Pretoria to Lourenço Marques (now Maputo) to give Transvaal an ocean outlet independent of the hated British. Rather surprisingly, the same 3ft 6in gauge was chosen, for one would not have put it past the devious Kruger to have chosen a different gauge just to prevent subsequent integration. Motive power policy seems to have been decided by the Württemberg firm of Emil Kessler of Esslingen, near Stuttgart, builders of some of the most quaint motive power of the late 19th century. To Kessler, *schmalspur* (narrow gauge) meant tank engines, so regardless of the fact that the 566km route from Lourenço Marques to Pretoria was much longer than any route served by the Württemberg State Railways with standard gauge and tender engines,

tank engines were supplied for South Africa.

By British standards, this was the equivalent of running the train service from London to Glasgow, over gradients which make Shap and Beattock look like billiard tables, with outside-frame 0–6–4Ts! Of course, Kruger and his consultants were technically naïve, and the service provided was certainly faster and more reliable than the only alternative, ox wagons on dirt roads, often rendered impassable in the rainy season.

The other constituents of the CSAR comprised the Pretoria–Pietersburg, the Selati, and the Imperial Military Railways, of which the latter was the largest and which served mainly parts of Transvaal and the Orange Free State using basically Cape and Natal type motive power. Faced with this amalgam of competent and weird motive power, P. A. Hyde, the first chief mechanical engineer of the CSAR, set about designing some very effective motive power, which followed two quite different forms. Possibly this was due to having two consecutive chief draughtsmen, but equally the two earlier designs were rapid stopgaps developed from the most effective inherited power. The best locomotives inherited must certainly have been the 8th class 4–8–0s of CGR design, featuring bar frames, narrow fireboxes, and cylinders with overhead slide valves actuated by inside Stephenson valve gear. What Hyde did in effect, was to produce a 4–6–2 version of the 8th class (later SAR class 9), for passenger service, and then extrapolate this to a 4–6–4T (SAR class F) for heavy suburban trains. Very likely the majority of renewable components were standard with the 8th class, despite which these two new classes had relatively short lives.

Hyde's real monuments were the SAR 11 and 10 classes, respectively 2–8–2 freight and 4–6–2 passenger, built in the same year (1904) as the 9 and 11 classes. Totally different to the other classes, they featured plate frames, wide fireboxes, and piston valves driven by Walschaerts motion. In other words, every major feature was changed! These sturdy and effective machines were renowned for their longevity, and the 10 class passenger 4–6–2s lasted until 1972, although by then downgraded to light duties.

More remarkable were the 11 class 2–8–2s built for the heavy coal traffic from Witbank to Germiston.

(above) *Trains from Lourenço Marques to Pretoria (566 kilometres) were hauled originally by outside-frame 0–6–4Ts such as this veteran, still working at a Transvaal gold mine in 1969. At least, they were faster than ox-carts!*

(below) *Unrebuilt class 10C No 776 accelerates out of Bloemfontein station in May 1968 with a suburban train to Melorane.*

Of the 36 locomotives built in 1904, no fewer than 13 were still hard at work in 1984, eighty years later! These survivors are not in SAR service, but have been sold into industrial use where their proportions seem just right. Some have even in the 1980s been fitted with air brakes in an evident policy of prolonging their lives yet further.

Hyde was succeeded by L. S. Smart, who produced no new designs, and was in turn replaced by G. G. Elliot who updated Hyde's Pacifics, firstly with inside admission piston valves (SAR class 10A), and later by superheating this design (SAR class 10B). The outside admission valves of the original Hyde locomotives gave a very free exhaust and to hear one of the veteran 2–8–2s, eighty years old, hammering away in industrial use, it is hard not to imagine that one is not listening to a modern, long lap locomotive, perhaps fifty years its junior.

A final design, basically of the Hyde type, was the class 10C small-wheel 4–6–2, delivered after Union. In the absence of any alternative design philosophy,

Around 1980 Tavistock Collieries built a new railway to connect its original line to SAR's Saaiwater yard. The line was built to main line standards, but 78-year-old class 11 No 1 still handles traffic in 1982.

these Hyde designs could well have formed the basis of future development, but this was not to be. Elliot, clearly aware as were his compatriots on the other provincial systems, of several advantageous features in American design, ordered two experimental locomotives from Alco, the class 10D 4–6–2 passenger, and the class MD 2–6–6–2 compound Mallet, itself an alternative to a previously purchased but unsuccessful 0–6–6–0 Kitson-Meyer. The Garratt, later to replace such machines, was evidently considered at the time to be insufficiently established as a possible competitor.

Cape Government Railways

The largest of the railways comprising SAR, Cape motive power policy had been very much 'British Colonial' in style from 1872 to the 1890s. Neat and delightful designs of 4–4–0, 2–6–2, 2–6–0, and 4–6–0 wheel arrangement proliferated, with variations as straight tender locomotives, full tank engines, and as tank tender machines. A curious feature of the CGR was its parsimony in allocating class designations, which in reality cost nothing, and it is difficult now to imagine why several quite distinct

classes came to be grouped under such designations as 'Cape 1st class'. As a matter of interest, the early 2–6–0 tender classes, some with horizontal cylinders and others with inclined cylinders, were virtually identical to similar machines supplied concurrently to the main 3ft 6in gauge systems in Australia.

In 1891 a pair of Baldwin 2–6–0s was bought to compare British with American designs under colonial conditions, and in 1897 six Baldwin 4–4–2 passenger engines built for Japan were purchased by the CGR. These added wide fireboxes to the bar frames of the earlier 2–6–0s as matters for consideration, and definitely turned motive power practice towards these directions. In the decade embracing the turn of the century, motive power as built was largely of four basic groups. The 6th class(es) group comprised six-coupled general passenger engines with 4ft 6in driving wheels. Most were 4–6–0s, the majority with plate frames, although some of both British and American build had bar frames. Also included in the 6th class were some wide firebox engines with trailing trucks—two 2–6–2s (SAR class 6Y) and eight 2–6–4s (SAR class 6Z), of which the first four were built as 2–6–2s. These

The Cape 7th class were the Southern Africa 'pioneer' locomotives, light enough to run anywhere. This one is at Ladysmith in 1970, at the end of its life. Two were still working at a coal mine in 1984.

2–6–4 tender engines were unique in the world as built, and only in 1908 did Gölsdorf in Austria build further examples of this type for express service. Nevertheless, the South African 6Z locomotives were clearly the pioneers of this new wheel arrangement, and Austria was the only other country to adopt it.

The Cape 7th series comprised the low-wheel 4–8–0s, with plate frames, possibly conceived as a freight version of the 6th class 4–6–0, but truly taking on the rôle of pioneer power, being highly suitable for rough pioneer tracks. In various forms they were supplied to much of Africa, for example Rhodesia, Angola, Congo, in pure form, and developed with superheaters and piston valves, to other countries. Their design stemmed from the successful application of eight-coupled power, in the shape of 4–8–2T, in Natal, and were virtually a 'tenderised' Natal tank design.

11

The Cape 8th group were mainly larger 4–8–0s with bar frames, classifiable as mixed-traffic engines. Basic features were very American, although all were British-built, and there were also some 2–8–0s with wide fireboxes. America came into the picture with two 2–8–0s having tandem compound cylinders, one with a narrow and one with a wide firebox. The 8th class in its normal form was also 'exported' to other African railways; a handful, long since rebuilt with new piston valve cylinders, are still at work in South African industry.

The other main Cape group was the 5th class 4–6–2s, known as the Karoo type, being intended for use over that dry region, and not used in other parts of Africa. However, Kitson, which built some of the type, used the design as a basis for a batch of 4–6–2s delivered to the Midland Railway of Western Australia.

All the above types were sound in both concept and detail design and owe much to the mechanical instincts of M. Stephens, CME from 1885 to 1895, and his successor, H. M. Beatty, who reigned from 1895 to the end of the CGR in 1910. Beatty was aware of the future and its needs for larger and more advanced power, and in 1903 had Kitson build a pair of 2–8–2s, of basically 8th class capacity, but with wide firebox supported by a trailing truck. Evidently successful, the design was enlarged to the maximum then possible, and a much larger 2–8–2 with 4ft 6in wheels (passenger size) supplied also by Kitson in 1906. Evolution may have seemed a little slow, but with long distances between user and builder, each new step had to be evaluated fully before further decisions were made. Equally, the CGR was reaching out into locomotive dimensions unprecedented at the time outside North America. In 1906 a freight locomotive with 55 tons adhesion weight, (72¼ tons total), 31,730lb tractive effort at 85 per cent boiler pressure and a grate area, wide firebox, of 33 sq ft were way outside the norms of Britain, India, and Australia on *standard and broad gauges*, let alone narrow gauges anywhere.

Having proved that such a huge locomotive could operate with success on the narrow gauge, an even larger 4–8–2 derivative was evolved, with a leading bogie to ease passage round curves, and the extra axle used to support a yet larger boiler with 37 sq ft grate. Two such locomotives were ordered and were delivered in 1911, by which time all was SAR. Rakish engines, with slide valve cylinders and

inside Stephenson link motion, and devoid of super-heaters, these SAR class 4 locomotives were very much the link between 19th century Cape detailing and 20th century high power dimensions. Rather remarkably, they were not the swan-song of Cape practice. As late as 1913–14, several years after Union, the SAR took delivery of ten class 4A, a development of the earlier locomotives, with super-heaters and piston valves. It seems hardly likely that such a design could have been placed before 1910 by the CGR, so one assumes that the final Cape design was actually ordered after formation of the SAR. The last working example of the Cape 4A, by then reboilered as class 4AR, was retired from industrial use at Apex Colliery as late as 1983.

Thus ends the purely South African story of these excellent 4–8–2s. However, Rhodesia Railways, looking particularly for a locomotive for the long Bechuanaland (now Botswana) section south of Bulawayo, accepted what must have been the North British Locomotive Company's proposal for what was to all intents and purposes a lighter version of the 4A. Many dimensions tally, including the slightly uneven coupled wheel spacing, and like the 4As, the RR 10th class had combustion chambers, the only RR locomotives so equipped. There is much more than coincidence between the similarity of designs, but the real truth is now probably shrouded in the mists of history.

Natal Government Railways

This system has been deliberately left to the last in this pre-Union survey as it was the NGR Chief Mechanical Engineer, D. A. Hendrie, who became the first CME of the new South African Railways, thus occupying this position for a total of twenty years, on two railways, and with a continuously progressive policy. Like the NZASM, the Natal system relied entirely on tank engines for the first three decades of its existence, the reason given being reduction of deadweight over the 1 in 30 gradients of the series of fierce climbs over the Zululand escarpment. Frequent halts for coal, water, and locomotive change must have been the order of the day; again with animal haulage over atrocious roads, the only competition was hardly a motivator of better overall speeds.

The tank engines used grew progressively in size, from the 25-ton 2–6–0Ts of 1876, the barely larger 4–6–0Ts of 1882, some of which were developed to 4–6–2Ts and even 4–6–4Ts, with increases in deadweight but not in power. In 1888 a 2–8–2 tender tank locomotive was built in the railway's Durban workshops, and this pointed the way to future practice, although not truly successful in original form. W. Milne was in charge of locomotive matters during this period, and his masterpiece was the class A 4–8–2T, of which 100 were built from 1888 to 1899. They were the first locomotives ever to have

(top left) *During its last year in service in 1983 Grootvlei's class 8DW No 3* Puffing Duggie *waits with a scrap truck at No 6 shaft. Note the narrow gauge cocopan undergound trucks in the background.*

(below left) *An early morning in 1977 on a cloudy summer day sees black class 4AR No 1559 piloting dirty red class 1 No 2 out of Greenside Colliery with high-sided coal wagons for the Highveld Steelworks at Clewer.*

This pair of NGR survivors, class 1 4–8–0s Nos 3 and 2 at Apex Colliery, are mere youngsters of 75, yet these sturdy Hendrie locomotives still perform heavy haulage for the coal industry.

(top left) The World's first 4–8–2s were these little Dübs tank engines built in 1888 for the Natal Government Railway. This one was discarded recently at Grootvlei Mine, Springs, and one final survivor is works shunter at Dunn's, Witbank.

(below left) Tavistock Colliery No 1 was the last class H2 in industrial service. It is seen with front tank plating removed for easier access to the motion. Also note the offset big-end, required by the eccentric main crankpin. The blanked-off horn gap clearly indicates the locomotive's original condition as a 4–10–2T.

the 4–8–2 wheel arrangement (tender engines followed tanks in this respect). One of these little engines was still yard shunter in 1984 at Dunn's Locomotive Works in Witbank, and it bids fair to achieve a century of service, as did one of the older 4-6-0Ts.

Milne retired in 1896, and was replaced by G. W. Reid, who continued the policy of tank engines, and went one stage further in specifying a 4–10–2T, which with heavier axle load gave over 50 per cent more power compared with the A class. Wisely only one was ordered for delivery in 1899, for there was no precedent available for such an enormous narrow gauge tank engine. Only the Mersey Railway and the Barry Railway in Great Britain had a few locomotives of similar size, on standard gauge, and even the Continent would have been hard pressed to find a competitor. Successful trials of the prototype led to the building of 100 further examples, plus 35 for the Imperial Military Railways during the Anglo-Boer war, and finally another for Witbank Collieries as late as 1927. The total of 137 locomotives built to this design was about double all the other 4–10–2 locomotives elsewhere in the world, all tender engines, and divided between the USA and

Hendrie's classic Pacifics of classes 16 to 16C worked passenger trains for 60 years. Here No 814, rebuilt as a class 16CR with Watson boiler, rolls into Nigel with a train from Springs in July 1967.

Brazil. Reid's 4–10–2T was therefore very much a pace setter.

Reid was succeeded in 1903 by D. A. Hendrie, who as chief draughtsman and later works manager of the Highland Railway in Scotland was probably largely responsible for the detail design and subsequent maintenance of the famous 'Jones Goods' 4–6–0s. It is reputed that Hendrie clinched his position due to 'experience with steep gradients', but the 1 in 60s and 1 in 70s of the Highland main line must have seemed like gentle undulations compared with the miles and miles of 1 in 30 which characterised the Natal main line. The first design attributed to Hendrie was an intermediate size 4–8–2T (SAR class G) which one suspects was designed and ordered by his predecessor, and simply commissioned in Hendrie's time.

That tank engines were not Hendrie's idea of how to run a main line railway soon became evident, and his first real design showed no backward glances towards earlier Scottish practices. Bearing in mind that Hendrie came from a rather small railway in the north of Scotland, far from the 'top ten' of British railways, his outlook concerning locomotive design was remarkable, to say the least. The Hendrie B, his

most numerous class, was a splendid 4–8–0 with outside cylinders, outside Walschaerts valve gear (almost unheard of in contemporary British practice, although much later to become standard), and a wide firebox. In Great Britain, the only wide firebox locomotives in 1904 were a score of Atlantics on the Great Northern Railway, about a dozen 2–6–0s and 4–6–0s on the Great Western Railway, and the solitary 'Decapod' 0–10–0T on the Great Eastern. Hendrie's 4–8–0, on narrow gauge, had more grate area than any but the 'Decapod', and by building 50 in the first batch, Natal immediately possessed more wide firebox locomotives than the whole of Great Britain! A further 21 were built in 1910.

Meanwhile, to ease riding on passenger duties, and possibly downhill tender first when used for uphill banking, Hendrie rebuilt six locomotives in 1906 as 4–8–2s, adding a pony truck under the cab. Thus the NGR not only invented the 4–8–2 type as a tank engine, but was also the first user of a 4–8–2 tender locomotive. The first 4–8–2 tender locomotives built as such were the New Zealand class X of 1907–8; these, like the Natal engines, had the grate over the coupled wheels. The first 4–8–2s with wide fireboxes totally behind the coupled wheels, which some purists maintain forms the pure 'Mountain' design, were also Hendrie engines, his class D (SAR class 3), of which 30 were built in 1909–10 by North British. An American version (SAR class 3A) was built for comparative purposes by Alco in 1909 with bar frames instead of the substantial plate frames of Scottish tradition. Two years later, having been prompted by a British colonial railway in darkest Africa, America 'invented' the 4–8–2 type and dubbed it the 'Mountain' type after the Chesapeake & Ohio Railroad Allegheny gradients which, while heavy, were nothing like the 1 in 30s of the Natal main line.

For passenger service on the easier sections, between Ladysmith and Charlestown on the Transvaal border opposite Volksrust, Hendrie built two classes of 4–6–2, each of two engines only. The A class, although placed in service a year after the B class 4–8–0s, was evidently an earlier design, and had inside Stephenson's valve gear, making it very much a 'Jones Goods' extended to a Pacific, with wide firebox. The second two engines, class C, were very slightly larger, and followed the B class 4–8–0 in having outside Walschaerts valve gear. SAR classed these Pacifics as 2 and 2C respectively, and

The only Hendrie class 14 never reboilered to class 14R was No 1750, seen towards the end of its life as Enyati Railway No 3.

it is interesting to speculate what they had in mind for the blank classes 2A and 2B!

South African Railways

Upon formation of the SAR in 1910, there were three main avenues of locomotive development, headed by Beatty of the Cape, Hendrie of Natal, and Elliot from the CSAR. Each had developed extremely effective designs for his own system, and any could have formed the basis for South African standard designs. Hendrie was chosen as the new Chief Mechanical Engineer, and for most duties he developed the basic designs, 4–6–2 and 4–8–2 already tested and found satisfactory in Natal. The greater SAR system featured longer distances and in many cases less arduous gradients than Natal but the Hendrie designs, developed in size and detail, coped extremely well.

For the principal passenger services, Hendrie built the 16 class 4–6–2 in 1914, and typically the class had more tractive effort than any British passenger locomotive of the day, and more grate area than all but the 4–6–2 No 111 *The Great Bear* of the Great Western Railway. Possibly influenced by Churchward's practice, Hendrie then produced a

Class 12s at Nigel. Early in 1973 class 12R No 1861 on the afternoon Heidelburg to Springs freight waits in the passing loop while class 12AR No 2105 shunts in the goods yard.

pair of four-cylinder simple expansion 4–6–2s, class 16A, in 1915, which were quite remarkable for 3ft 6in gauge. However, while these apparently ran very smoothly, they had less tractive effort than the two-cylinder class 16, and whereas the SAR loading gauge permitted greater development with two cylinders, the rail gauge prevented enhanced power using four. As was standard on Hendrie engines, both classes had superheated Belpaire boilers, and piston valves actuated by Walschaerts motion. On the four-cylinder locomotives, which had cylinders in line but divided drive, the inside valves were worked from rocker arms ahead of the cylinders, which may have caused problems due to expansion of the outside valve spindles, while there was a substantial difference in the connecting rod length, and the angularity therefrom. Possibly these cancelled out each other, leading to the smooth-running reputation of the 16As.

Further Pacifics were the ten 16B of 1917–18, with larger cabs but mechanically identical to the 16 class, followed by 30 class 16C of 1919–21, which had fireboxes including combustion chambers. By this time, the SAR had some 54 Pacifics of modern design on the 'narrow' gauge compared with Great Britain, the mother country, which had but one, although some more were in course of construction.

For other duties, SAR was much more ahead than British design as regards sheer size. For freight duties in general, and mixed-traffic use over heavy

gradients, Hendrie developed his Natal class 3B 4–8–2, in both size and detail, so that it became his recognisable masterpiece. For most of steam's reign on SAR, the 4–8–2 was the standard wheel arrangement, and the most numerous in use, whether in tank or tender form, or in later days as used in pairs under Garratt articulated locomotives.

Development of the Hendrie 4–8–2 is difficult to arrange in a coherent pattern of narrative. The purely chronological system produces rather a jumble, and it is perhaps more convenient to take them in groups, especially as the first group includes all the major variations. For the heavy coal traffic between Witbank and Germiston, over what to Hendrie were easy gradients of about 1 in 80, or slightly less than Shap, the 3B class with 3ft 9in wheels was developed into a heavier locomotive with 4ft 3in wheels and larger dimensions throughout. These were class 12, built from 1912 to 1922, and numbered 46 examples. Dimensionally similar, but with larger cabs, were thirty class 12B of 1920 built by Baldwin to British design, including plate frames. All these class 12 and 12B locomotives were very much to the 3B design, and included cylinders with 'Z'-port indirect steam passages.

It was later realised that superior performance could be achieved with cylinders having more direct ports, and although Hendrie's designs never advanced to the completely straight ports already in use by Churchward twenty years earlier, his later locomotives did move towards more modern cylinder design, with straighter ports and larger steamchest volume. The class 12A built from 1919 to 1929 had these improved cylinders, plus boilers with combustion chambers. Dimensions were also enhanced to the point where they had greater tractive effort not only than Gresley's class P1 2–8–2 mineral engines, but Riddles' final Class 9F of a quarter century later! Boiler dimensions, including 40sq ft of grate area, were fully commensurate with the 12A's cylinder power.

In Hendrie's days, it was thought that small variations in wheel diameter made significant differences to locomotive performance; hence with only six inches' difference between the wheel diameters of the 3B and 12 classes it was thought worthwhile for mixed-traffic duties in Natal to introduce the intermediate 14 class, with 4ft 0in diameter wheels. Excellent engines, they were not only intermediate in size but in design features, having the straighter port cylinders later used on the 12As, but not the combustion chamber. Sixty class 14s were built, and these were followed by 41 lighter locomotives of class 14A, with smaller boilers and cylinders. Fifteen of the 14s, originally classed 14B, were built without superheaters, but this was soon found to be a false economy, and rectified.

For mixed-traffic work across the easier gradients of the Orange Free State and the Northern Cape lines, Hendrie produced what was his masterpiece, the 15 class, in 1914. Using the more modern cylinder design combined with a wheel diameter midway between the 12th classes and the 16th classes of 4–6–2, these 4–8–2s were very much 'universal' locomotives. Certainly, both quantities built and longevity confirm this statement, for they comprised Hendrie's most numerous class—today,

70 years after the first was built, the majority remain in service! The first ten formed class 15, without combustion chambers, and were built in 1914. In the same year came the initial batches of class 15A, with combustion chambers, and production continued until 1925, by which time there were some 129 of the combined series. Most of the 15A had a larger and wider design of cab, supported on a straight running plate, but the first batch had the narrower cab and dropped running plate of the earlier Pacifics. One of each 15A version remained unaltered and both may be preserved.

Transatlantic versions

In the years immediately following World War I, South Africa was beset by a serious locomotive shortage which traditional suppliers were unable to satisfy rapidly. Capacity was available in Canada, and contracts were placed with the Montreal Locomotive works to supply versions of both the 14 and 15A classes of 4–8–2. Unlike the American firms of Alco and Baldwin, which were familiar with plate frame locomotives in their export business, Montreal had only built bar frames before, and with speed of building essential it was agreed to accept these. Bar frames were nothing new to SAR, since it inherited many such engines from the CGR.

The last narrow-cab class 15A No 1791 pilots class 15CA No 2828 into De Wild station on the Pretoria–Rustenburg pick-up train in September 1969.

The daily Queenstown–Burgersdorp 'washout' turn, double-headed with class 15AR locomotives, is seen towards the end of its run with the late afternoon sun bringing out the best of the rugged Karoo scenery.

Accordingly both classes were redesigned in Canada, retaining only the key Hendrie overall dimensions. Even the fireboxes were redesigned, tapering down towards the backplate, a probable improvement. The main design difference was in the bar framing, and since this involved cylinders cast integrally with half saddles, the opportunity was taken to provide larger and straighter steam ports, and piston valves having longer travel, but retaining short steam lap. The net result was in two designs having noticeably sharper and choppier exhausts than the Hendrie originals, this being evident even after all were later rebuilt with Watson standard boilers. Some 73 of the class 14C were built, divided into 14C, 14CB, and 14CM variants, while 30 larger wheel engines were class 15B. At the same time, north of the border, Rhodesia was experiencing a similar locomotive supply problem, and thirty 4–8–2s were supplied by Montreal as

RR class 11th, essentially a lighter version of SAR's class 14C.

Articulated locomotives

South Africa, with its steep gradients and sharp curves, is a natural country for articulated motive power, and as the limitations of eight-coupled straight engines began to be approached it became imperative to find some means of increasing tractive effort on steep gradients without resort to costly double heading. It is interesting to note that the 25NC class 4–8–4s of 1953 had only 7½ per cent more adhesion weight than Hendrie's 12A class of 1919.

(top right) *An over-view of East London station and carriage sidings in December 1976, with class 14CRB on shunting duties.*

(below right) *For a while during the early to mid 1970s, Randfontein Estates ran miners' passenger trains from Cooke 1 shaft to the Millsite complex. Old SAR suburban coaches were used. A train hauled by class 15BR No 1 is seen against a backdrop of mine tips.* Christine Durrant

South Africa's first sortie into articulated power was a couple of double Fairlie 0–6–6–0Ts, built by Avonside in 1875 and 1878. The small firebox with inadequate grate area, plus cramped firing conditions inherent in the Fairlie design led to their abandonment and eventual scrapping in 1903. They were used in the Eastern Cape, apparently mainly on the short steep haul up from the docks at East London. They were tried out against a pair of 'back-to-back' 0–6–0Ts which are not true articulateds, but were no more successful. It was not long before straight 4–6–0 tender engines were developed with equal power and far greater convenience and reliability than these early articulateds.

The year after the Fairlies were scrapped, another articulated made its appearance, this time the Kitson-Meyer. Now the Kitson-Meyer has many good features, and in South America was developed into a useful and reliable type of motive power. Not so the African version, an 0–6–6–0 with coal on board the locomotive but water carried in a conventional tender coupled behind. Cylinders were at the rear of each bogie, those on the trailing bogie exhausting through a separate chimney behind the cab. This final feature, by denying the blastpipe half the exhaust steam, probably accounted for the type's reputation for poor steaming. Short-wheelbase bogies with outside cylinders gave a rough ride, detracting further from their popularity. Had the tender's water supply and four axles been transferred to the locomotive, making it a 2–6–2 + 2–6–2T, and the rear exhaust diverted through the main chimney, the result would have been useful enough for development into an eight-coupled version of considerable effectiveness. As it was, the engines as built were even on paper no more powerful than the eight-coupled tender engines then being successfully introduced in the country, comparative dimensions being tabulated below:

Date	Railway	Class	Type	Tractive effort (lb @ 75%)	Grate Area (sq ft)
1903	CGR	Exp 4	2–8–2	24,370	27
1904	CGR	Exp 5	2–8–2	28,000	33
1904	CSAR	(SAR 11)	2–8–2	30,870	37
1904	NGR	B	4–8–0	31,240	34
1904	CGR	Kitson-Meyer	0–6–6–0T	34,560	34

Altogether, four of the Kitson-Meyers were built, one each for the CGR, and for the CSAR, and two for Rhodesia. None lasted even a decade, the CSAR being the last survivor, in 1912.

The Mallet Era

It was that remarkable man Hendrie who was responsible for the introduction of the Mallet to South Africa. A bar-framed compound articulated was a far cry from anything experienced on the Highland Railway, but doubtless that canny Scot had witnessed the failure of the Kitson-Meyers, and was too much of a realist to dally further with the Fairlie concept. British technical periodicals of the day, notably The Engineer, were full of detailed accounts, complete with general arrangement drawings, of 'The largest locomotive in the World', and from 1904 onwards these were all massive Mallets of American construction. Accordingly, Hendrie went to the USA to see what Mallets were all about. North British had yet to build its first Mallet, and discussion would have been difficult in the two European countries which possessed Mallet tender locomotives of adequate size with six-coupled units — Spain and Russia!

Upon return from the USA, Hendrie had placed orders with the American Locomotive Company for an experimental 2–6–6–0 Mallet plus a bar-framed 4–8–2 for direct comparison with his own class D 4–8–2s. Not surprisingly, when NGR No 336 was delivered in 1909, it was the largest and most powerful narrow gauge Mallet in the World, with an engine-only weight of 86½ tons and tractive effort, compound, of 44,810lb. That same year, 1909, there appeared the World's first Garratt, as yet a tiny and untried experiment, but which was to develop and eventually oust the Mallet from South African rails.

Having spotted a potential market, the Alco salesmen were quick to respond, and the CSAR had its first Mallet just one year later in 1910, a 2–6–6–2 somewhat larger than Hendrie's, but clearly with many components in common. At 100¾ tons, it was the first South African locomotive to exceed 100 tons engine-only weight. Equally it was the first 100-tonner, not only in the southern hemisphere, but outside North America.

Upon the formation of SAR in 1910, a renumbering and classification of locomotives was started, in which Mallets were allocated classes beginning with M, the original Natal locomotive becoming MA and the CSAR class MD. No further class MA were built for SAR, although two virtually identical locomotives were built for the Lourenço Marques railway in Moçambique; these are believed to be still in existence, derelict, in the wilds of the Zambezi valley at Moatize. The class was developed, five more Alco versions with larger boiler being class MB of 1910, while ten similar but heavier machines came from North British in 1912, as class MC. Finally another batch, again slightly heavier, of 15 class MC1 was supplied by North British in 1914,

(top left) Baldwin-built Mallet of class MB, lettered SAR but carrying an NGR number.

(centre left) Superheated Mallet class MC1 No 1642 at De Doorns shed, from where it banked trains over the Hex River Pass.   South African Railways

(below left) Class MF compound 2–6–6–2 No 1629. South African Railways

Class MF Mallet as rebuilt with four simple-expansion cylinders. South African Railways

making 31 compound 2–6–6–0s of which the fifteen MC1 were superheated as built. Two of the MC were later superheated. All these 2–6–6–0s were originally used mainly on heavy banking work in Natal, but the 1925 electrification made many redundant, some being transferred to the Witbank–Germiston coal run and others for banking on the Hex River Pass, these probably being the last to go. The MBs were finished by 1925, being outlived by the solitary MA by two years. The MC soldiered on until 1933, and the MC1 until 1938.

Meanwhile, the CSAR class MD 2–6–6–2 was also being developed and fifteen further 2–6–6–2s were delivered by Alco in 1910–11. Fourteen of these, class MF, were a superheated version of the MD, while class MG was an experimental machine having larger wheels on the low pressure unit than on the high, in an effort to combat sluggishness. In addition, it had a Street mechanical stoker of Heath Robinson complexity and was unsuperheated. The mechanical stoker was soon removed. These locomotives were used mainly on the Witbank–Germiston coal traffic, where their sluggishness was more evident than in the Natal banking batches. Six were converted to simple expansion in 1923–25, although no new diagram or classification was issued to cover this modification. Some, including three of the simplified engines, were transferred to the Eastern Cape for the East London main line, and of the three classes the MD lasted until 1926, the MG until 1927, while the fourteen MF were slowly phased out between 1930 and 1939.

We now come to the largest and smallest Mallets

— the final development for heavy coal traffic, and the three branch line classes. Class ME was a solitary 2–6–6–2 simple expansion superheated Mallet, built by North British in 1912, long before simple Mallets became commonplace in the USA. Its axle load was under ten tons, and the cylinder and wheel dimensions were those very successfully used later on the GC and GCA Garratts and FC 'Modified Fairlies'. Presumably the class would have been multiplied eventually, but for the Garratts, and as a 'one off' it had a respectable life until 1937, on the Nelspruit–Sabie branches.

For the heaviest coal traffic between Witbank and Germiston, five enormous 2–6–6–2s, class MH, were built by North British in 1915. At 128¼ tons apiece without tenders, they were again the largest locomotives built outside North America. After displacement from the Witbank coal line, they shifted to the Glencoe–Vryheid route, for similar coal haulage, and were withdrawn during 1938–40. It is interesting to note that by then SAR's largest Garratt and Mallet classes were working the same line, although no photographs seem to exist of the two classes together.

The last and longest-lived of SAR's Mallets were the MJ and MJ1 branch line 2–6–6–0 superheated compounds, of which the 18 class MJ were built by Maffei and North British between 1914–21, the most numerous Mallet class. The eight MJ1 were built by Alco in 1918, and dimensionally were almost identical. All 26 locomotives remained intact until 1947. In March 1948, when the capital stock was 16 MJ and eight MJ1, the active figures

SAR's largest and most powerful Mallet, class MH. Author's collection

showed ten MJ and five MJ1 in the Eastern Cape, plus four MJ in Natal. The Natal locomotives are believed to have been used on the Eshowe branch, and the Cape Eastern allocation gradually whittled down to two in 1962, the Amabele–Umtata line through the Transkei being their last stamping ground. Thus the reign of the Mallet in SA ran 53 years from 1910 to 1962. The total number of Mallets built was 79, but only in 1921 were all in stock.

The Transvaal and Delagoa Bay Collieries, Witbank, became users of the last Kitson-Meyer, No 1600, together with MA No 1601, MB Nos 1605/6, MC No 1614 and MC1 No 1643. The colliery with all its locomotives was closed before anybody seemed interested in photographing such things, but the MC1 tender survived and was last used with a GM Garratt at Douglas Colliery.

Enter the Garratt

Having first introduced the Mallet to South Africa and developed it to virtually the practical limit of the time, Hendrie was quite open-minded concerning its limitations. A good puller at low speeds, the Mallet of those days was a sluggish machine and developed to anything much larger than an MH would have severe throwover problems accentuated by SAR's narrow gauge and sharp curves.

The Garratt promised to alleviate these problems, and in 1914, before delivery of the MH class, a decision had been made to order Garratts for trial. At this time most of the few Garratt designs in service were on 2ft 0in or 2ft 6in gauges, although some 17 Garratts had been built for 3ft 6in gauge on two railways in Australia. Cautiously, five were ordered, three being for the railway's 2ft 0in gauge lines, and one, not so much larger, for lightly-laid branches on 3ft 6in track.

The fifth locomotive was something quite different indeed! Designed apparently as a direct competitor to the MH, it closely duplicated the Mallet in terms of tractive effort, boiler capacity, grate area, and axle loading. The result was a locomotive of equal power yet 46 tons lower in weight, of which 11 tons were accounted for by the empty boiler weight and several more tons by less water in the boiler. The rest must have been simply due to the greater clumsiness of a Mallet with separate tender — more framing, additional wheelsets and so on. On Natal's 1 in 30 gradients, the sheer reduction in deadweight will have allowed more than ten per cent additional train loading, or conversely more economy hauling similar loads. All this came about, the Garratt being more economical than the Mallet, while it was also faster over the test sections, mainly due to faster downhill running; the large low-pressure, slide valve cylinders of the Mallet inhibiting free running. It was sufficient to prove the case, and no more Mallets were ordered for SAR. However, Hendrie realised that where conditions do not dictate an articulated type, a straight engine is more economical, and his unfulfilled *magnum opus* was a 2–10–2 proposal for the Witbank coal traffic.

25

The Collins Period

After the retirement of Hendrie in 1922 eighteen years after he came out from Scotland to the NGR, the post of chief mechanical engineer was taken over by Colonel F. R. Collins, who held it until 1929. Unlike Hendrie, who produced a similar number of basic classes covering two railways, plus a difficult wartime period when new classes had to be obtained from unusual suppliers, Collins produced no fewer than 22 locomotive classes (of which 13 were articulated) in only seven years! One cannot help but think that Collins must have viewed a new locomotive class with the sort of delighted anticipation that a Sultan faced a new and exotic contribution to his harem!

Hendrie's locomotives were recognisable as such—without having seen a drawing of his proposed 2–10–2, one knows just what it would have looked like. Conversely, there was no such thing as a recognisable Collins design. Evidently the practice under his chieftainship was to send out a general specification to tender and choose what seemed the most attractive offer, leaving detail design to the manufacturer. As an occasional policy, to bring new ideas into a stodgily run department, it has much to commend it. As a standard policy for a major railway system where things like the quantity, variety, and cost of a stores inventory are taken seriously, such a multiplicity of classes with little in common reeks too strongly of a small railway in a banana republic owning twenty locomotives of fifteen classes, supplied by eight builders from six countries, and kept in more or less working order by a chief mechanic who trained on agricultural machinery!

This does not say, of course, that the locomotives produced under Collins' name were all bad. Far from it—responsible major locomotive builders faced with an opportunity to serve a 'new' major customer generally give of their best unless prevented from doing so by restrictive specifications. Circumstantial evidence points to Collins having funny, Midland Railway-type ideas on cylinder design and valve events (Collins was trained in Crewe, England), preventing some designs from being as good as they might have been. Certainly, the later Hendrie cylinders were better than many of Collins' introduction.

If the proof of the locomotive is in its length of service, it is interesting to observe that one of Collins' classes remains in service almost intact on SAR while members of six other classes remain in service to industry. For a man who retired 60 years ago, it is not a bad record.

In dealing with Collins' locomotives, chronological order creates confusion, and it is best to deal with them under sub-headings of service requirements. For main line services, full credit must go to the Baldwin Locomotive Works, USA, for designing and building the two classes which proved to be the basis for SAR main line steam design for the next 30 years. There had long been a suspicion that for South African conditions of long distances coupled with heavy gradients and primitive servicing facilities, American locomotive practice could prove more relevant than British (the delicate complexities of European practice not even being considered). Even Hendrie, when ordering his first Mallet had bought an American 4–8–2 for comparison with his own, while post World War I had forced upon him the delightfully free-running 14C and 15B classes. There must be something to it!

Hence from Baldwin were ordered two heavy 4–8–2s to class 15C, and two corresponding Pacifics of class 16D, each designed to the then maximum limits permissible on SAR, while the maximum number of components was interchangeable between the two pairs of engines, probably more for Baldwin's convenience than to Collins' specification. The 4–8–2s were immediately dubbed 'Big Bills', and their passenger counterparts 'Big Berthas'. Scaled down in size, but not in proportion from the rugged machines used in the USA, they proved an instant success in South Africa, and were followed by repeat orders of five Pacifics and ten 4–8–2s, the latter being reclassified 15CB.

As tends to happen with the rather immoral promiscuity of 'Big Business', Baldwin's original design work guaranteed them no more than one smallish repeat order for each type. Thereafter, the design at the rear end was modified from the straight-through frame under the firebox to something approximating to the earlier Hendrie and Hyde designs, with built-up widened frames under the firebox, giving more room for the ashpan. This was a serious consideration for a narrow gauge locomotive, where between-frame space is at a premium, and with Baldwin's arch rival Alco credited with the new design it became 15CA—or that is what we are told today. The 15CA proved equally efficacious as the 15CB, and Alco got an order for 23 of the new class, while Baldwin, the originator received a derisive four locomotives. That was not all—Breda in Italy, which had never built anything like it nor anything so huge, got ten locomotives, while just to prove that blood is thicker than water (or steam) North British was given the largest contract for 47 locomotives. The second batch of NBL locomotives built in 1930 had cabs tapering slightly inboard above the waistrail, and one or two earlier locomotives received these cabs retrospectively, probably as a result of rectifying collision damage. The 15CA have proved themselves excellent locomotives, being extremely surefooted. Short-lap valve gear was fitted, but rather surprisingly long-lap, long-travel gear was never applied, although this could have been done inexpensively. Probably the reason was the well known industrial disease of 'accountantitis', which refuses to spend

Class 15CB No 4 leaves Brakspruit shaft in 1981 with loaded ore hoppers for the Rustenburg Platinum Mines plant at Waterval.

the penny which will save a pound. This is usually countermanded by 'politicianitis', which then spends ten pounds in a vain attempt to save what originally would have cost a penny. Of course, the politician makes more *baksheesh* from ten pounds than he would from a penny. The 15CA locomotives remain mostly at work today, relegated to shunting, where their short-lap valve gear at last justifies itself in strong starting, and to hell with efficiency.

Collins' express engines, the 16D and 16DA Pacifics were basically a six-coupled version of the 15Cs, with slightly larger wheels. They differed only in the rear end arrangements, the seven 16Ds corresponding to the 15CBs, and the fourteen 16DAs corresponding to the 15CAs. At the time of introduction, they were by far the most effective of SAR express engines, outshining even the Hendrie Pacifics, although they would have been even better with more modern valve events. Surprisingly, they were never modified, but several 16DAs were sold into colliery work, where their short-lap valves ensured good slow-speed operation.

Collins' other main line type was the class 18,

three-cylinder 2–10–2 for the Witbank coal traffic. This was probably a belated development of Hendrie's ideas for such a machine, and as built was undoubtably a bold design, even if it lacked state-of-the-art detailing, and had questionable proportions. Two were built by Henschel in 1927, and contemporary Henschel publicity refers to them as the 'Henschel Giants'.

Giants they certainly were, being larger in most dimensions than Deutsche Reichbahn's new class 44 three-cylinder 2–10–0s, although the all-up engine weight was almost identical. Clearly, on a narrower rail gauge, items such as axles and frame stretchers are shorter, saving weight which can be built into other items, for example the firebox. Henschel had long experience in building three-cylinder 2–10–0s for Germany, which is probably why they got the order. The company had produced hundreds of the Prussian G12 and G12[1] locomotives, and was

awarded the first batch of 44 class. Nevertheless, there were several features which Henschel would probably have discarded had it been given a free hand in the design.

Firstly, the wheel diameter of 4ft 9in was larger than any of the German types on standard gauge. At that time 4ft 9in was the mixed-traffic size for SAR as used on the 15th classes of 4–8–2; six inches smaller would have allowed a 2ft shorter coupled wheelbase, greatly easing passage through SAR's sharp curves. Secondly, cylinder design with narrow tortuous ports was a backward step from the later Hendrie designs, and even further back from

Easter 1976 saw the Pietersburg–Tzaneen passenger train double-headed by a splendid class 15CA plus 15F combination, seen here winding through the forested hillsides near Duiwelskloof.

German main line practice which for many years had featured long-lap, long-travel valves, in straight port cylinders; SAR was the first railway in the world to standardise such features, followed closely by Churchward on England's Great Western Railway.

Gresley gear for the inside valve was perhaps understandable. Prussia had tried and discarded the earlier type of conjugated gear as later adopted by Gresley, and the 44 class had a neat arrangement with a sort of mini cranked axle providing the primary movement for the centre valve motion. There is far less room between bar frames on a narrow gauge locomotive than on standard, making Gresley gear even more attractive. Holland states that it gave much trouble with wear and breakage, but no attempt was made to replace it. The 18 class hauled 1,800-ton trains from Witbank to Germiston, rather more than the 1,600 tons allocated to the

(top left) *Near Fouriesmith in 1972 standard and wide firebox class 16DA double-head the Bloemfontein–Bethlehem daily train. The two Pacifics were arranged specially by the Railway Society of Southern Africa at the time when these classes were being withdrawn from service.*

(below left) *The classic American wedge shot – it could have been on the Illinois Central Railroad – but the heavy 4–8–2 is a South African class 15CA, and the bogie hoppers are destined for the coal mines at Witbank from the Pretoria line.*

A pair of East London class 19A locomotives, Nos 685 and 694, double-head a Transkei freight train through Komga station on 10 October 1969.

Mallets. It is interesting to compare the dimensions of the 18 class with the German 44 class 2–10–0, also with the later 45 class 2–10–2 express freight locomotives for the same railway, and these are tabulated below. The boilers on the 18 class were round-topped, had fireboxes with combustion chambers, and arch tubes supporting the brick arch.

Railway	SAR	DR	DR
Date built	1927	1926	1937
Gauge	3′ 6″	4′ 8½″	4′ 8½″
Locomotive class	18	44	45
Locomotive type	2–10–2	2–10–0	2–10–2
Cylinders (3)	21¼″ × 28″	23·6″ × 26″	20·5″ × 28·35″
Wheel diameter	4′ 9″	4′ 7″	5′ 3″
Boiler pressure, lb/sq in	215	199	284
Tractive effort, lb, at 75%	53,650	58,930	60,355
Grate area, sq ft	60	50·6	54·3
Locomotive weight, tons	114·55	112·3	126·4
Adhesion, tons	92·5	97·8	97·8

In numerical order, Collins' next design was the class 17, which was no more than an A class 4–8–2T with rear end removed and replaced by a tender, becoming a 4–8–0 tank-plus-tender, similar to but smaller than the earlier 13 class.

For branch line work over lightly-laid track, hitherto carried out by various types of 7th and 8th classes of 4–8–0, by then getting somewhat long in the tooth, Collins introduced the 19 class light 4–8–2 with axle load limited to 13½ tons for use on 60lb/yd track. They were lighter in total weight and in axle load than any Hendrie 4–8–2 and set a new standard for branch line power; their descendants will stay in service to the end of SAR steam. With bar frames, and short-lap valve gear they were very much a smaller and lighter version of the 15C class. Only four of the original 19 class were built, followed in Collins' time by the marginally smaller 19A class, details of which will be found in the locomotive classes section.

Another innovation by Collins was the use of purpose-built shunting engines instead of the prevalent practice of using time-expired and often unsuitable main line engines for this service. Here Collins followed American rather than

30

European practice in the use of a tender engine design—the 0–8–0, or 'eight-wheel switcher'. Designated S for shunter, they were built by Henschel, and with wide fireboxes and 4ft 0in driving wheels, approximated roughly to the old Prussian G9 class as later superheated. As was so often the case, the SAR version on 3ft 6in gauge was larger than the original on standard. The S class was followed by S1 and S2 developments, and again set a new standard.

On balance, the tender engines introduced by Collins, while not truly excellent by worldwide standards, were distinct advances on previous types, and the 15C, 19, and S classes set definite standards which were followed by subsequent chief mechanical engineers until the end of steam construction for SAR. It was unfortunate that the 18 class was not more successful, for this contained the genes, inherited from Hendrie, of where SAR practice should have proceeded.

Collins' reputation was tarnished by the extraordinary number and variety of articulated designs which proliferated under his aegis. Upon taking office there were numerous Mallets still in service, while two 3ft 6in Garratt designs were proving better. There were probably still memories of the recently defunct Kitson-Meyers. Collins apparently became something of an articulation enthusiast, and at one time stated that this was the locomotive of the future. Perhaps he was right, as all recent acquisitions have been double-bogie machines, although electric or diesel!

With the Garratt proving so successful, several 'jump-on-the-bandwagon' alternatives were propounded by companies anxious to utilise the Garratt's good features without paying royalties to Beyer Peacock. They found in Collins a willing ear and, more important, a pen ready to sign contracts. Two major deviations from the Garratt norm were produced, the first being the so-called 'Modified Fairlie' which was in essence a Kitson-Meyer in having two power units, sufficiently spread apart so that the firebox was slung between. Instead of the usual side tanks, the 'Modified Fairlie' had the boiler frame cantilevered out forward to hold a front tank, to make it look like a Garratt. All this did was to increase loads on the main pivots, and reduce deadweight on the engine units, leading to increased maintenance and poorer riding in service.

Beyer Peacock itself was partly responsible for the second variation on a theme by Garratt. The unsuccessful New Zealand machines had the coal bunker rigidly mounted on the main boiler frames, allegedly to make mechanical stokers easier to apply. Down in Bavaria, engineers at J. A. Maffei, perhaps recovering from a particularly heavy *Oktoberfest*, cross-bred the rear end of a 'Modified Fairlie' with the front unit of a pure Garratt to breed a new hybrid. A brilliant stroke of PR named the bastard creation the 'Union-Garratt', and Collins signed on the dotted line. Two types of 'Union-Garratt' were produced, and so confused were the requisite authorities (having perhaps been invited to the next *Oktoberfest*) that a schizophrenic decision was made, one class being allocated G for Garratt, and the other U for Union!

Altogether, five classes of these pseudo-Garratts were ordered by Collins in addition to eight classes of real Garratts which should be dealt with first, as these were mainly direct derivatives of Hendrie's Garratts. From the original class GA were developed the GE 2–8–2 + 2–8–2s, of which 18 locomotives of three variants were built during 1924–30. These survived into the 1970s, and are dealt with in the class survey of this book. For passenger work, the solitary GG 2–6–2 + 2–6–2 was built in 1925, but was not repeated. Both the GA and GG locomotives carried boilers interchangeable with the GE, and when the solitary locomotives were scrapped, these boilers went into the spares pool.

A class U 'Union Garratt'. Kelland Collection, courtesy Bournemouth Railway Club

Class FD 'Modified Fairlie' No 2323. North British Locomotive Co, courtesy SAR

For branch line work Hendrie introduced the class GB, with eight-ton axle load for the lightest branches, and although introduced during the Collins régime the similar but larger classes GC (12-ton) and GD (13-ton axle load) were probably originally outlined by Hendrie, having his standard features of plate frames and Belpaire fireboxes. From these basic Garratt designs Collins, who preferred bar frames and round-top fireboxes, not only developed alternative Garratt designs with these features, but also on the same basic wheel arrangements and axle loadings had versions supplied to the 'Modified Fairlie' design. The various classes concerned are tabulated below in order to obtain a clearer picture than words can convey:

| Basic Garratt | | Developed Garratt | | Modified Fairlie | |
Class	Quantity	Class	Quantity	Class	Quantity
GC	6	GCA	39	FC	1
GD	14	GDA	5	FD	4
GE	18	–	nil	HF	11

Class HF 'Henschel Fairlie' No 1386. SAR

The sum of this endeavour was 98 locomotives divided into no fewer than eight different classes in order to cover only three traffic requirements. The confusion was such that the eight-coupled 'Modified Fairlie', which should logically have been class FE, became HF for 'Henschel Fairlie'.

On top of this lot came the two classes of 'Union Garratt', of which one received a Garratt classification (GH) and the other its own designation, class U. Again, logically, they should have been classes UA and UB. The class GH comprised a pair of heavy 4–6–2 + 2–6–4 passenger engines, which as proper Garratts could have been developed into something really useful. The class U were 2–6–2 + 2–6–2s of slightly greater size than the GE Garratts, but with a much heavier axle load. It is difficult to imagine just what their introduction was meant to achieve. In the long run all these pseudo-Garratts were scrapped much earlier than their straight Garratt alternatives, having proved less satisfactory in both operation and maintenance.

Two further Garratt proper classes came out under Collins, and these proved very useful and long-lived designs. Class GF was a light 4–6–2 + 2–6–4 of similar axle load and general capacity to the same designer's 19 class 4–8–2, the Garratt being about ten per cent more powerful. Sixty-five were

built in Germany in 1927–28, all giving over 40 years' sterling service, with a few being still at work today on the Enyati Railway in Natal, almost 60 years on.

The final Garratt produced under Collins had a long gestation period, having been first proposed during Hendrie's régime. One suspects that it was a Beyer Peacock proposal schemed out in order to demonstrate the potential capacity of a large Garratt, perhaps as an alternative to electrification. The design was a large 4–8–2 + 2–8–4 on an 18½-ton axle load and the original scheme, published in *The Railway Gazette* for August 1922, shows a very Hendrie-type design, complete with Belpaire firebox and plate frames. After the Natal electrification was under way there came a stop-gap need for such an immense Garratt, to eliminate double-heading of 14 class in hauling the same loads as three electrics of class 1E. Developing no doubt from the original diagram, Beyer Peacock built in bar frames and a higher-pitched boiler with round-top firebox, essentially of the originally designed capacity, but with a larger superheater.

Dunn's class GF No 2404 hauls a rake of CCL air-braked coal wagons for loading, along the Enyati Railway in 1981.

Mechanically, connecting rods were lengthened to drive on the third coupled axle, and larger straight port cylinders were included. For the first time on SAR, long-lap piston valves were included, set with cut-off limited to 65 per cent in full gear. The first two machines were an instant success, and were quickly followed by a further six. The locomotives spent their lives in Natal, only shortly for their original stop-gap main line duty, while over 30 years were spent on heavy coal traffic between Vryheid and Glencoe Junction, where their rated load was 1,240 long tons up gradients of 1 in 50, some for several miles on end; this required a continuous exertion of about 75,000lb tractive effort, considerably exceeding their designed specification for hauling similar loads on a mere 1 in 66. In many ways, the GL class set a design standard followed later by the GM, GMAM and GO classes, and it is a pity that further Garratts of maximum size were not built.

33

African miners at Nos 3 and 6 shafts at Grootvlei Gold Mine, Springs, are treated daily to rides in vintage wooden rolling stock, headed by a rare steam locomotive that would delight the heart of the enthusiast. Here class S 0–8–0 No 1 King Kong propels its train past No 3 shaft, homeward bound to the residential compound.

The Watson Era

Colonel Collins resigned in 1929 and was replaced by Mr A. G. Watson who, unlike his predecessor, had very firm ideas as to how locomotives should be designed. Watson laid the foundations upon which most later SAR designs were based. Watson's main cornerstones were very wide Wootten fireboxes with large grate area, and poppet valves, for his main line types. For maintenance reasons, he favoured boiler standardisation, and where possible he increased wheel diameters as it was thought at the time that this decreased wear and tear. For the heaviest duties he favoured ten-coupled non-articulated loco-motives, and was opposed to Garratts or other articulated types, perhaps as a shock reaction to Collins' profligacy in this field. Watson was the only CME who went in for extensive reboilering of older

classes, using two basic standards, the No 1 boiler, 5ft 0in diameter and made in two lengths called 1 and 1A, to suit various locomotives. There were also the 5ft 7½in diameter Nos 2, 2A, and 2B. These five boilers were fitted to about 20 classes of locomotive, effecting economies in workshop costs, but appar-ently in some cases reducing steaming capacities where plain round-top fireboxes replaced former Belpaire boxes with combustion chambers. Watson followed Germany's Dr Wagner in favouring fire-boxes without combustion chambers, mated to boiler barrels with long tube lengths, having high re-sistances to gas flow. In the absence of sophisticated exhaust systems, good steaming was achieved by heavy blasts and high back-pressures, making de-lightful noises for steam enthusiasts but leading to high coal consumption.

Watson also fitted superheaters and piston valves to many older locomotives of classes 7 and 8, while some 8 class locomotives (designated 8W, 8AW etc.) also had modern cylinders with straight ports and long-lap, long-travel, valves. These modern cylin-ders were also applied to the older 4–6–2s of classes 5 and 5B, whether or not fitted with new standard

At Annandale on the now-electrified line to Harrismith class 15E No 2875 heads west with a freight train, piloted by class 19D No 2673.

Class 16E No 856 makes an impressive exit from Bloemfontein with a Sunday local passenger train to Springfontein in August 1967.

boilers as classes 5R and 5BR, but it seems unclear how many were rebuilt with the new cylinders.

Watson's express locomotives were quite outstanding. Six class 16DA which were probably already on order or in a late stage of adjudication when he took office were completed with his prototype wide fireboxes, with 60sq ft of grate area. These led the way to the next six 4–6–2s, the splendid 16E

In 1978 the Cape Town Branch of the RSSA ran a fine trip to Ceres, using the last class 19C, No 2439. Emerging from the mountains, the train is seen approaching Wolseley on the return journey.

class with 6ft 0in driving wheels and rotary cam poppet valves, among the most remarkable locomotives to run on less than standard gauge.

For mixed-traffic work, the 16E cylinders and wide firebox boilers were fitted onto basically a 15CB chassis to form the class 15E heavy mixed-traffic 4–8–2, of which 44 were built. For lighter mixed traffic on secondary lines, Watson took delivery of the class 19B, a basic Collins design, and had built 50 of his own version, class 19C, with rotary cam poppet valves. These three Watson poppet valve classes, 15E, 16E, and 19C thus totalled exactly 100 locomotives.

Ten-coupled designs

Since articulateds were anathema to Watson, something had to be done about services where ordinary six- or eight-coupled designs were inadequate, and his remedy was to use ten-coupled tender engines.

This was already common practice in continental Europe and the USA, but South Africa had then a very British railway system, and treated ten-coupled types with considerable caution, there being another couple of decades before British locomotive engineers found out how easily such machinery could be made to go round corners!

The first ten-coupler was the solitary class 20, assembled in Pretoria workshops from a 19A boiler, 19C cylinders and motion, and wheels from withdrawn 8th class locomotives. The resulting 2–10–2 could be considered the designer's answer to the GCA Garratt, having very similar weight and tractive capacities, summarised below:

Class	GCA	20
Type	2–6–2 + 2–6–2	2–10–2
Tractive effort, lb, at 75%	28,470	33,080
Grate area, sq ft	34	36
Axle load, tons	11·8	11·7

The tender engine had more water and coal than the Garratt, and weighed about twenty tons more. The design was not repeated or modified by his successor.

36

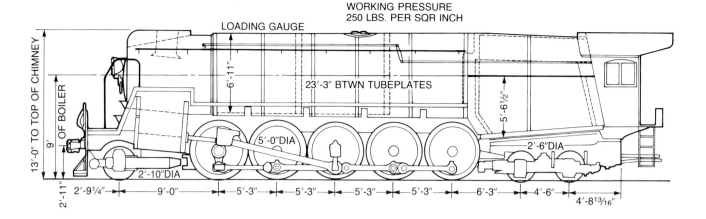

WORKING PRESSURE
250 LBS. PER SQR INCH

LOADING GAUGE

13'-0" TO TOP OF CHIMNEY

9' OF BOILER

6'-11"

23'-3" BTWN TUBEPLATES

5'-6½"

5'-0"DIA

2'-6"DIA

2'-10"DIA

2'-11"

2'-9¼"   9'-0"   5'-3"   5'-3"   5'-3"   5'-3"   6'-3"   4'-6"

4'-8¹³⁄₁₆"

Watson's second ten-coupled design, class 21, was a mixed-traffic machine to run on 60lb/yd rails, and with 4ft 6in wheels, and an axle load less than 15 tons, it could be compared with the GF Garratt, in a similar manner:

Class	GF	21
Type	4–6–2 + 2–6–4	2–10–4
Tractive effort, lb, at 75%	34,200	43,700
Grate area, sq ft	44	63
Axle load, tons	14·45	14·95

The 21 class weighed 23 tons more than the Garratt, and carried more water only. As designed it would also have had rotary cam poppet valve gear, having the same boiler as the class 15E, but being completed by Watson's successor it had long-travel piston valves instead, similar to the 15F class.

Neither of these designs was subsequently multiplied in original or modified form, which is a pity, as they represented advanced thinking which seems to have frightened-off subsequent CMEs. Neighbouring Moçambique had several classes of ten-coupled locomotives, supplied and used over a long period with complete success, such that it is clear that no fundamental problem exists in running modern ten-coupled designs on Cape gauge. Across the Atlantic, both Argentina and Brazil also made a complete success of similar locomotives on metre gauge.

Watson's *magnum opus* was unfortunately still-born, and consisted of the immense class 22 2–10–4 with a 22-ton axle load, representing the heaviest that current SAR track could bear. The design was a compromise between a 2–8–4 passenger class with 5ft 6in wheels, and a 2–10–2 freight engine with 5ft 0in wheels, the proposal sketches of which have been recently unearthed. Watson retired before anything could be done about this locomotive, which seems to have frightened the wits out of his successors! The reason given for its non-production was that it was a freight-only design, whereas mixed-traffic locomotives were really required. On a railway whose main line trains are 90 per cent freight this sounds

Watson's proposed 22 class 2–10–4 with 22-ton axle load and 80 sq ft of grate area.

more like a feeble excuse, and certainly the existence of a fleet of locomotives of such capacity, if of different design, is exactly what SAR needs today.

Like Watson's other designs, the class 22 proposal had poppet valves, a huge boiler with 80sq ft of grate, 250lb/sq in boiler pressure, (a figure never attained on an SAR locomotive) and large cylinders inclined to clear the loading gauge in a manner reminiscent of the much later British Railways Class 9F, which later was a bantam-weight by comparison. Watson retired in 1936, and was succeeded by W. A. J. Day.

The Day Period

Day was chief mechanical engineer only from 1936 to 1939, but was clearly a very sound engineer. While not aspiring to Watson's creative high-flying, he placed in service some of the most popular and trouble-free locomotives the SAR has seen. Again, he tended to build on previous practice, and in turn that was used as a basis for those who followed him, continuing a process of steady evolution. His main cause to fame was in recognising, rather belatedly in South Africa, the value of long lap, long-travel piston valves driven by robust Walschaerts valve gear.

Of nearly 3,000 steam locomotives owned by SAR, only the eight GL Garratts and the handful of rebuilds from classes 5 and 8 had these features, which Day proceeded to apply with a vengeance. First of all, the 19th class of branch line 4–8–2 was so re-designed, with the result that class 19D became the most numerous and popular branch line engine on the SAR, some 235 being built under and after Day's tenancy as CME. For main line work, he replaced the poppet valves on Watson's 15E design and created his 15F, identical except for the provision of long-travel piston valves. This was the most successful of all SAR classes in quantity and popularity, some 255 being built. Only 64 of these were built during Day's tenancy, as he then developed the

37

design to the class 23, with larger wheels and higher boiler pressure, and although these were very good engines they never quite attained the popularity of the 15F. The 23s suffered from frame fractures, probably due to their being built in Germany during 1938–9. One may imagine that in those immediately pre-war years, Germany's best steel was going into armour plating for tanks and battleships, leaving export locomotives with material which in all probability barely met the minimum specifications.

On a clear summer's morning in 1973 a class 15F is seen at Fouriesburg on the overnight Bloemfontein–Bethlehem passenger train, passing through rocky hills typical of the region.

Unlike Watson, Day had no inhibitions about using Garratts, and his fourth design was the class GM 4–8–2 + 2–8–4, devised to clear a bottleneck which had developed on the line from Johannesburg to Mafeking, lightly laid with 60lb/yd rail, yet having long gradients of 1 in 40, and carrying all traffic between the Witwatersrand and Rhodesia. A variety of power was in use: GE and GF Garratts, various 19th classes of 4–8–2, and Watson/Day class 21, 2–10–4. The best acceptable combination of motive power was a pair of 19th class, and using as a basis two 19D chassis and a shortened GL boiler Day schemed out what was to be the basis of the World's most useful and numerous Garratt class. Only sixteen class GM were produced just before the

38

war in 1938–9, but they certainly proved their worth subsequently, and became the design basis for the later GMA/M and GO classes.

Dr M. M. Loubser, 1939–49

Dr Loubser had a longer reign than his two predecessors, but it was a reign that embraced the wartime period of make-do-and-mend, so that if he had any bright ideas on advanced designs there was little or no opportunity to produce them. Compared with those who came before, with their numerous designs, Loubser had to be content with four new classes, yet he initiated, as always, something of value which was used later.

The Hendrie class 12A locomotives were becoming due for reboilering, and as none of the Watson standard boilers would fit the bill, Loubser had designed a new but larger boiler on similar lines. The resulting rebuild, class 12AR, *looked* much larger and more massive than the original 12A, but this was largely an optical illusion. With the elimination of Hendrie's Belpaire firebox with combustion chamber, a reasonable firebox volume

The last class 12AR to remain in service was No 1535 Susan, the Germiston station pilot. Here the old lady belies her 60+ years by blasting out of Grootvlei in 1983 with an RSSA 15-coach special.

could only be obtained by pitching the boiler much higher, which was done, resulting in a locomotive which looked much more massive than the original, but was in fact only four cwt (0·2 tons) heavier in terms of the official diagram book, and perhaps lighter or heavier in everyday practical reality.

The second design which came out under Loubser's name was the GEA Garratt, whose designation probably started out as the never used class GN. Fifty of these were ordered immediately after the war, and were delivered during 1946–47, the largest single Garratt order ever placed with Beyer Peacock. In theory an enlarged GE, only the basic boiler dimensions tallied with that class. Some 30 years of very hard work was done with this class, one of the largest designs of Garratt to be hand fired.

During the war shunting power was at a premium, and Loubser had the class S redesigned to use a boiler which was effectively a shortened 12AR

39

unit. Twelve were built by Salt River Works in 1947–48, and a further 25 later ordered from North British. These massive shunters were in a class of their own, and resembled a Garratt boiler sitting on eight wheels. As a heavy outside-cylinder 0–8–0 they were suitable only for pure shunting work and no more were built, practice reverting to the use of downgraded main line locomotives which also could be used for local trip workings and even the odd main line turn.

Two classes introduced by Loubser paved the way for further development. Firstly there was the class 24, a lightweight 2–8–4 with maximum axle load under 12 tons, designed for use on track of 45lb/yd. Despite this limitation, the boiler was the standard

(top left) After piling on the coal during the downgrade run, and creating plenty of smoke in the process, a class GEA is opened-up fully for the climb to Botrivier on the Caledon–Cape Town route.

(below left) On the Lothair branch a pair of class 24 2–8–4s accelerate a bulk grain train from the Burgerspan water stop in November 1983.

Male ostriches are not noted for their friendliness towards humans, and despite its 'gricing' attitude this one is probably more interested in the intruder with camera than with the class 19D approaching on the morning passenger train approaching Oudtshoorn.

Type 1, shorter only in the barrel to that on the 19D class, and raising the conjecture as to how much better a boiler could have been fitted to a 19th class had the wheel arrangement been reversed to 2–8–4. The main feature of interest in the 24 class was the provision of a one-piece cast bed frame with integral cylinders, the success of which led to this feature being incorporated on subsequent main line and Garratt locomotives.

Loubser's other innovative locomotive was the conversion of the solitary class 20 2–10–2 into a condensing engine, with tender and equipment supplied by Henschel from Germany. With South Africa's generally dry climate, especially in the semi-desert Karoo region, a condensing locomotive offered substantial operating advantages in being able to cover long distances between water stops. On trial runs, the 20 class condenser was able to run some 600 miles (nearly 1,000 kilometres) between water stops, far exceeding the range of its coal bunker. Henschel had considerable experience in condensing locomotives, using a system applied as early as 1933 to a Russian 0–10–0 and developed in a substantial number of 0–10–0s and 2–10–0s built in Russia for the arid regions of southern Russia. During World War II some 200 of the wartime K52 2–10–0 were built with condensing gear for use in the German invasion of Russia. Also before the war six condensing 4–8–2 of metre gauge were built for the Argentine Central Northern railway.

Evidently the condensing 20 class was sufficiently successful to look promising, for it was subsequently included in the class 25 main line 4–8–4, introduced by his successor. Loubser retired in 1949, but it is interesting to note that his son later also became the chief mechanical engineer and, not stopping there, eventually rose to be General Manager of SAR, but sadly was to preside over the programme to replace steam traction.

Class 25 4–8–4s in straight and condensing versions team up at Hamilton in 1973 to work a Bloemfontein to Kimberley freight train.

L. C. Grubb, 1949–54

Grubb was the last CME responsible for the introduction of new steam locomotive classes, although his designs continued to be ordered and built by his successors. Three major types are attributable to Grubb, of which the first, class S2, was a lightweight 0–8–0 built to replace aged 4–6–0 and other locomotives used for shunting at docks and elsewhere. Very useful little engines, they were withdrawn prematurely and replaced in some cases by older but larger locomotives having more power for the heavier traffic offering.

Grubb's main achievements were the complementary classes 25 and 25NC 4–8–4s for main line duties. Specifications for these started off as an extended class 15F with larger boiler, and to test the effectiveness of a combustion chamber a class 23 was so fitted, with good results. The features which added greatly to the design's success were the integral cast-steel bed, already tried and tested on the class 24, and the application of roller-bearings to all axleboxes, crankpins, crossheads and return cranks. The ninety class 25 featured Henschel condensing gear as tried on the 20 class, and the fifty class 25NC locomotives were non-condensing, but

In this 1981 scene the Saturday 'Bombela' from Bethlehem to Ficksburg accelerates out of Sekonyela siding on the start of the return journey. The leading locomotive of the pair of class 25s is No 3405.

wherever possible identical. Even the cast frames of the 25NC had exhaust passages arranged suitably for conversion to condensing engines, although in the event, the opposite conversion was subsequently carried out.

Good though they were, several features on the 25 classes limited their effectiveness compared to what they could have been. The biggest drawback was lack of adhesion, the adhesion weight being the same as the heaviest batch of class 15F, even though tractive effort and steaming capacity on the class 25 were seven and ten per cent higher. The easiest way would have been to arrange weight distribution to give a 21-ton axle load as already used on class 16E, thus raising the adhesion factor from 3·67 to 4·15, using tractive effort at 75 per cent working pressure, as is SAR practice. Alternatively they could have been designed as 2–10–4s, which in view of SAR's predominantly freight haulage rôle would have been even more effective.

Something of the kind must have been passing through minds at the time, for North British schemed out a kind of super-15F with the same diameter boiler as a 25NC, rather less grate area, and a 4–10–4 wheel arrangement giving 27 per cent more adhesion weight than the eventual 4–8–4. About the same time, North British schemed out an 0–10–0 shunter, as a sort of super-S2, possibly at the time when contractors were having difficulty in fitting the original S2 specification into the required weight limits. Diagrams of these interesting proposals are shown on pp 44–5.

Nevertheless, the 25 classes have been outstandingly successful compared with other SAR tender engines, and as will be read later in this book have proved themselves more economic than diesel traction, in their unrebuilt form, and substantially so as rebuilt to class 26. Certainly they rank amongst the largest unarticulated locomotives to run in the southern hemisphere, being exceeded only by a handful of broad gauge designs in South Australia, Brazil and Chile, none of which were built in quantity, as well as 37 4–8–2s in New South Wales.

It is interesting to note that in 1945, several years before preliminary work on the 25 class commenced,

43

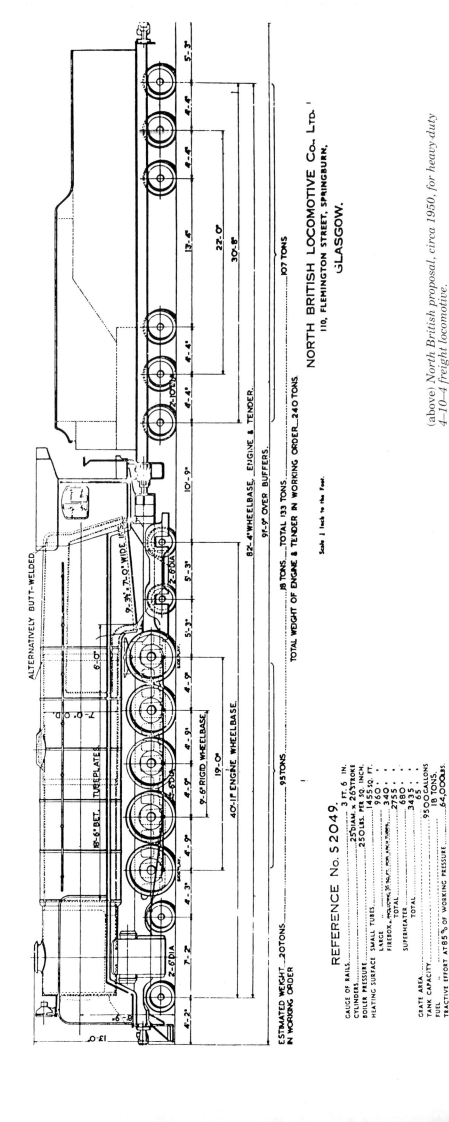

ALTERNATIVELY BUTT-WELDED.

REFERENCE No. S 2049.

GAUGE OF RAILS		3 FT. 6 IN.
CYLINDERS		25"DIAM. x 26"STROKE
BOILER PRESSURE		250 LBS. PER SQ. INCH.
HEATING SURFACE SMALL TUBES		1455 SQ. FT.
	LARGE "	960 "
	FIREBOX " INCLUDING 35 SQ. FT. FOR ARCH TUBES	340 "
	TOTAL	2755 "
	SUPERHEATER	680 "
	TOTAL	3435 "
GRATE AREA		65 "
TANK CAPACITY		9500 GALLONS
FUEL		18 TONS.
TRACTIVE EFFORT AT 85% OF WORKING PRESSURE		64,000 LBS.

ESTIMATED WEIGHT 20 TONS.
IN WORKING ORDER

95 TONS.

18 TONS. TOTAL 133 TONS.

TOTAL WEIGHT OF ENGINE & TENDER IN WORKING ORDER 240 TONS.

91'-9" OVER BUFFERS.

82'-4" WHEELBASE, ENGINE & TENDER.

40'-1" ENGINE WHEELBASE.

9'-6" RIGID WHEELBASE.

18'-6" BET. TUBEPLATES.

30'-8"

22'-0"

107 TONS.

NORTH BRITISH LOCOMOTIVE Co., Ltd.
110, FLEMINGTON STREET, SPRINGBURN,
GLASGOW.

Scale 1 Inch to the Foot.

(above) North British proposal, circa 1950, for heavy duty 4–10–4 freight locomotive.

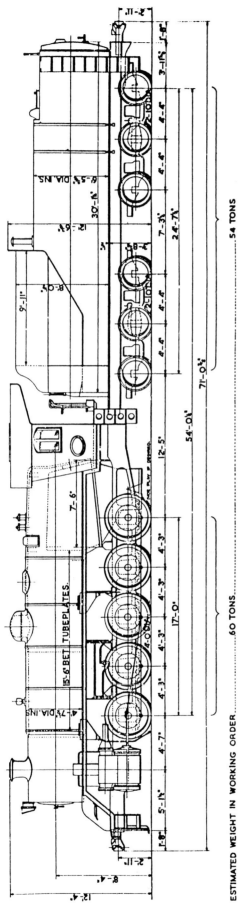

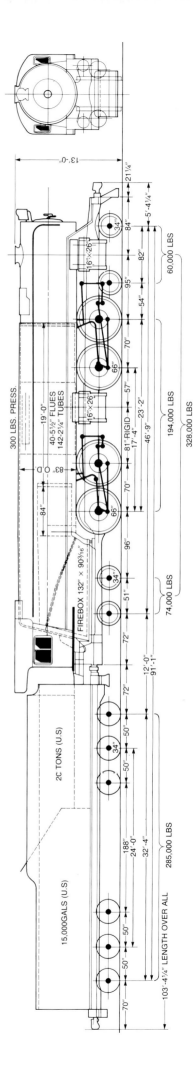

(above) *North British proposal, circa 1950, for 0–10–0 light axle load shunting locomotive.*
(below) *Alco proposal in 1945 for 4-4-4-4 Duplex locomotive, for SAR.*

Big power on the coal mine. Durnacol's class GM, trailing an old class 1 tender for extra water capacity, charges under the main road with a load of coal for the SAR interchange sidings at Dannhauser.

the American Locomotive Company produced a design for a 4–4–4–4 'Duplex' for SAR. This was an immense machine, with estimated weight even more than Watson's proposed class 22 2–10–4, and with 5ft 6in wheels was very much a passenger engine. At that time the 'Duplex' type was being built in fairly large numbers for the Pennsylvania Railroad in the USA, and it is interesting to note that such a design was prepared for South Africa, although the author has been unable to discover whether the initiative came from the railway or the builder. Certainly, in view of the type's lack of success across the Atlantic, it is fortunate that such machines were not actually built for South Africa, where good adhesion has always been of paramount importance.

Grubb's other major success was the re-design of Day's class GM Garratt into a more modern machine with cast-steel bed frames, and roller-bearings on all axles, although not on the crank-pins. Three ver-

sions were built, between them totalling 145 locomotives, by far the most numerous of any Garratt built. Like the GM, they were designed to work with a separate water tank car, only a small amount of water being carried on the locomotive itself. One hundred and twenty locomotives were to the GMA or GMAM designs, with all main dimensions tallying with the pre-war GMs. The difference between the two types was in the amount of coal and water carried, the GMA class having slightly more than the older GMs, and sharing with them the ability to run on rails of 60lb/yd. By altering baffles in tanks and bunkers, more supplies could be accommodated, making the engines slightly too heavy for light rail, hence the suffix M indicating main line use only. Over the years, there were in fact many conversions firstly from GMAM to GMA and later in the reverse direction, providing a fairly powerful locomotive convertible to run on light or heavy track as required.

Again, several disadvantages to this scheme became apparent especially in later days. A class GMAM was nominally equal in capacity to a pair of 19D tender engines, having slightly less tractive effort and boiler capacity, balanced by a reduction in total weight. However, even with small tenders, a pair of 19D would have 20 tons of coal capacity compared with 14 tons for a GMAM or 11·6 tons for a GMA Garratt, leading in some cases to running out of coal. Furthermore, although the GMAMs were only allowed to run on 80lb/yd track, their 15·7 ton axle load was nearly three tons less than that track could bear, and it seems now in retrospect that much better usage in total could have been achieved had about half the Garratts been built as GMA for lighter track, and the other half as much larger machines to utilise the capacity of heavier track. Such may have been a modernised class GL or similar.

The third type of these modern Garratts was the class GO, which with smaller boiler and cylinders was built down to an axle load of 13½ tons. Again, these Garratts probably never ran on track laid so lightly, and spent most of their short lives working over track capable of supporting much heavier and more powerful locomotives. The class GO worked only for just over 20 years, and spent the best part of another ten years rusting away in the 'strategic reserve'.

After the retirement of L. C. Grubb no new designs were prepared, although further examples of classes GMA/M were built. At one stage, the North British Locomotive Company was invited to set up a steam locomotive works in South Africa, rather on the lines of Chittaranjan works in India, but unfortunately the company declined on the basis of there being insufficient demand to make the plant viable. In view of the large numbers of electric and diesel locomotives which have been assembled and

In the last two weeks of steam operation over the Lootsberg Pass class GMA/M No 4051 emerges from the gorge at Jagpoort with a southbound freight.

Spotlighted by the sun setting over high mountains, a class GMA/M Garratt climbs Lootsberg Pass with the local pick-up freight from Bethesda Road to Rosmead.

The Sunday afternoon passenger train from Empangeni to Gollel approaches Mtubatuba after crossing the Umfolozi River, seen behind the train. The locomotive is a class GO, behind whose front tank can be seen the bridge in the distance.

partially manufactured subsequently in South Africa, this seems a short-sighted decision. Certainly, with an indigenous factory, new steam locomotives would have continued to be built for a much longer period, possibly until the present day. After 1958 the only new steam supplied were eight Garratts for the 2ft 0in gauge built by Hunslet Taylor of Germiston, Transvaal, in 1968. Two new classes appeared by rebuilding, the solitary 19R in 1967, and the class 26 of 1981.

Twilight and decline

Non-steam traction in South Africa commenced in 1925, when the first electrified section of the Natal main line was energised. Electric suburban services grew around the main centres of Johannesburg/Pretoria, Durban and Cape Town, and in the 1930s two small diesels were acquired for shunting duties, to see what advantages this form of traction possessed. They were not repeated. South Africa is a natural country for steam traction, having enormous deposits of inexpensively mined coal, and no oil. Electrification can be justified in areas of high density traffic, generating power from locally mined coal.

As a developing country, South Africa has not suffered the decline in traffic experienced in many parts of the World, and in general traffic levels continue to increase. Extensions of the electrified network really only got under way in the mid-1950s, and main line dieselisation, then sensibly restricted to areas with water supply problems, starting with South West Africa, got under way just before 1960. The maximum number of steam locomotives recorded in the annual report of the general manager was 2,755 in 1959, almost the same as the total number of locomotives in 1950.

Up to 1970 the steam stock dwindled slowly. Traffic build-up largely absorbed the new electric and diesel locomotives, and apart from the withdrawal of older and less powerful locomotives, steam displaced by other traction forms was concentrated on the remaining steam routes. The late 1960s were probably the highlight of steam in South Africa, with busy steam routes and lots of double-heading in all sorts of combinations—where there was steam it was thicker on the rails than ten years previously, when slightly more steam was spread over much more trackage.

49

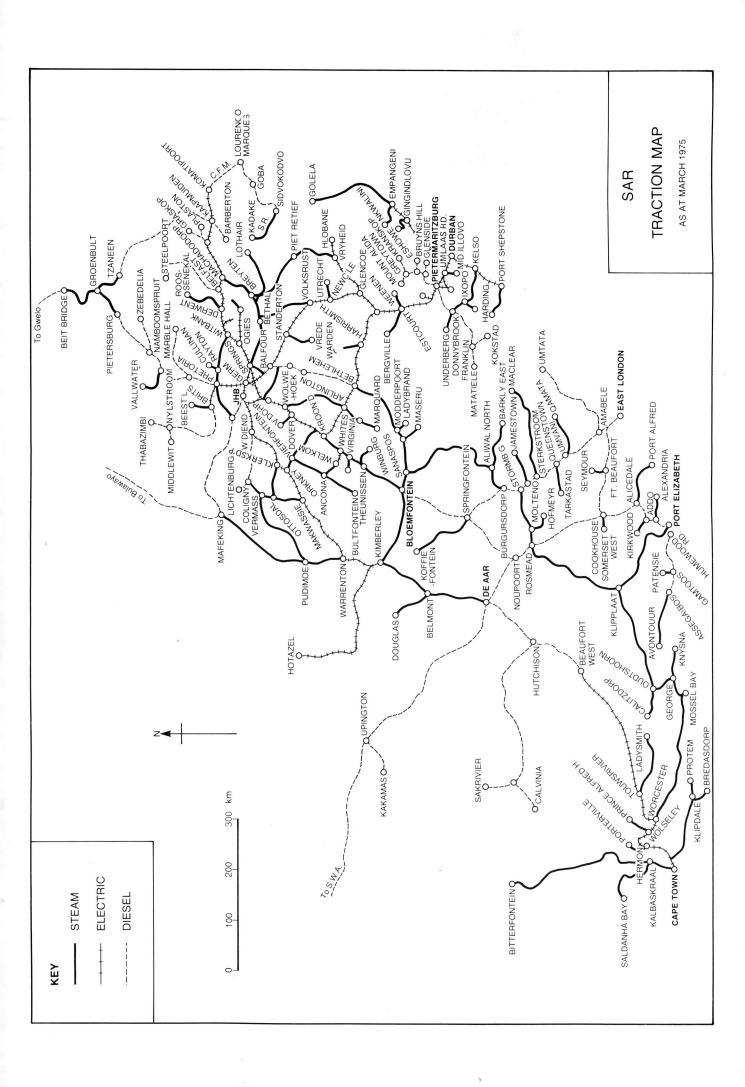

SAR
TRACTION MAP
AS AT MARCH 1975

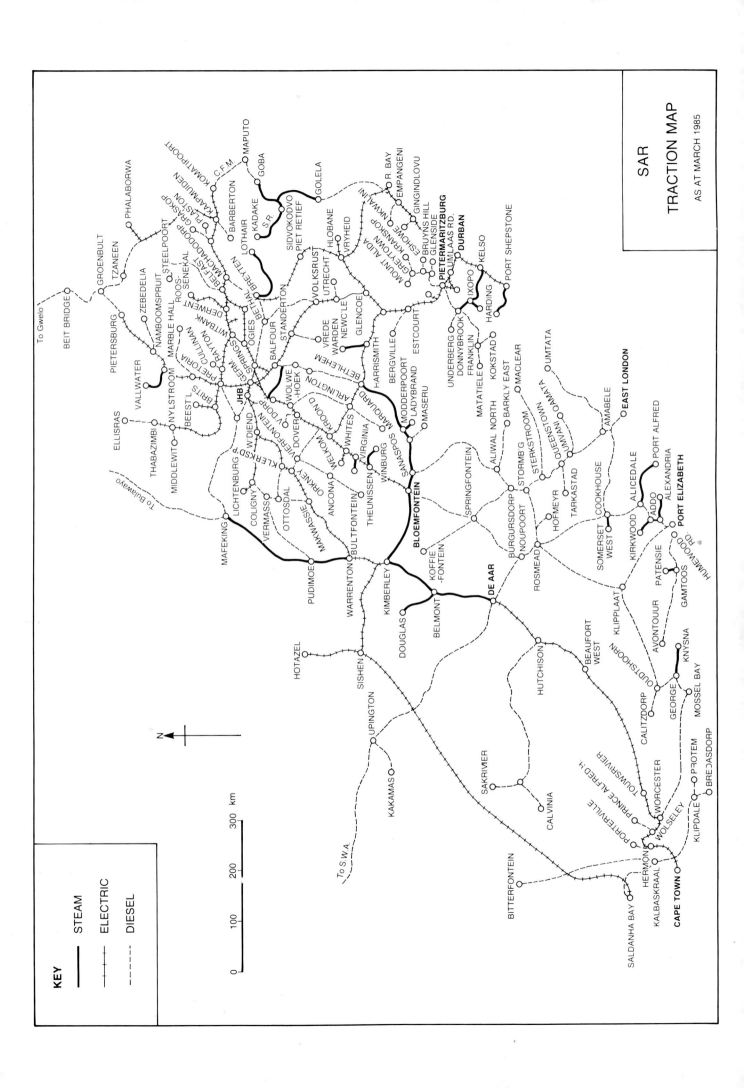

KEY

— STEAM

+++ ELECTRIC

- - - DIESEL

SAR

TRACTION MAP

AS AT MARCH 1985

Graveyard in the wilderness. Numerous class 19C and class S2 locomotives, withdrawn from service, rot at Touwsrivier. They were part of the 'strategic reserve' of steam locomotives, set aside to fool gullible politicians and public alike. The locomotives have since been cut-up.

In 1970 there was definite talk of the replacement of steam, by 'about 1987'. Senior railway management had become infatuated by the diesel, despite the fact that alone of the three traction modes it was entirely dependent upon imported fuel. With pro-diesel executives in the driving seat, all sorts of quite ridiculous 'reasons' were given for the replacement of steam, and these are detailed in Chapter 8. In the early 1970s the world oil crisis started to emerge, but SAR blindly continued to dieselise. The South African Government exhorted industry and the private individual to save oil, and clamped down on the supply of petrol for motorists, but the self-brainwashed SAR management totally ignored its government's call. Indeed, upon the fall of the Shah of Iran (South Africa's main oil supplier), one of SAR management's first moves was to order 200 more diesels!

By the late 1970s, even the diesel-infatuated management realised that rapidly rising oil prices were getting out of hand, and an enormous crash programme of electrification was instituted, regardless of the fact that most of the single track routes on the programme could never carry sufficient traffic to amortise the enormous capital costs involved. The most economic form of traction—new and modern steam locomotives—was religiously ignored except by one junior engineer at Pretoria. The net result, in terms of locomotives in capital stock is briefly summarised in the table below:

Year	Steam	Number of locomotives Electric	Diesel	Total
1950	2,540	216	2	2,758
1960	2,742	472	76	3,290
1970	2,473	1,112	379	3,964
1980	1,702	1,911	1,375	4,988
1984	900	2,250	1,601	4,751
1985	775	2,198	1,635	4,724
1986	695	2,334	1,599	4,628
1987	575	2,361	1,531	4,467
1988*	445	2,351	1,512	4,308
1989	250	2,344	1,398	3,992

*Note: 1988 figures are as at end February and 1989 figures as at 31 January; all other figures as at end March. The same applies to detailed class lists in Chapter 2.

SAR Locomotives Class by Class

During the preceding chapter on development there have been many references to classes which will be unfamiliar to those who have not visited South Africa. Upon the formation of SAR from its constituent systems in 1910 a general reclassification of locomotive stock was instituted, and this followed the following plan:

Unarticulated tender locomotives. Numerical basic class, with alphabetical designation for variations on a theme, *viz* 12, 12A, 12B etc.

Unarticulated tank locomotives. Alphabetic basic class with numerical variation designation, *viz* H, H1, H2, etc.

Articulated locomotives. Alphabetic letter denoting articulation type, *viz* M for Mallet, G for Garratt, etc., followed by second letter denoting class thereof, *eg* MA, MB, etc., or GA, GB etc.

Secondary variations numerical for Mallets, viz MC1, but alphabetical for Garratts, *viz* GEA, GMA.

Shunting locomotives. S with numerical variation, *viz* S1, S2.

Tertiary variations. R denoted locomotive rebuilt with standard boiler, *viz* 12R, 12AR etc. Loco-motives with weights lightened for branch line service, or increased for main line service, were respectively suffixed B or M, *viz* 14CRB, 14CRM, GMAM.

Narrow (2ft 0in) gauge. Separate series prefixed NG, commencing at class NG1. Garratts classed NGG within same series, for example the sequence NGG14, NG15, NGG16.

The following pages detail locomotive classes still in SAR service in 1973, together with building details, usage distribution, and annual quantities. Older SAR classes still in industrial service as at 1973 are omitted. Locomotives sold or preserved are individually noted.

The class designation is shown on the cabside number plate, whose oval surround includes an interesting microcosm of South African political history. Earlier the plates simply had SOUTH AFRICAN RAILWAYS. At a later date this appeared on the top of the plate, with SUID AFRIKAANSE SPOORWEË below. Later again the Afrikaans designation appeared above, with the English below!

Classes 1 and 1A 4–8–0 Ex-NGR 'Dübs B' locomotives

These sturdy old locomotives were quite remarkable machines at the time of building. Designed for main line freight and passenger work on the 1 in 30 gradients of Natal, they boasted twelve wheels (eight driving) wide fireboxes on a boiler 5ft 7in diameter, and outside cylinders with Walschaerts valve gear—all this at a time when the average British goods engine was an inside-cylinder, narrow-firebox 0–6–0 of about half the tractive effort! The only difference between a class 1 and a class 1A was that the latter had steam reverse, although some of the class 1 were later so fitted. The final six class 1 were built as 4–8–2 with an 'afterthought' pony truck under the cab, but these were later removed.

Apart from an early experiment with piston valves, the 'ones' remained saturated, slide valve engines for the whole of their long lives. Withdrawal commenced in 1935, but in March 1972 half the class, by then nearly 70 years old, were still in capital stock, the last only being written-off in 1975. However, in their last years few were at work, and as at April 1973 there were three at Mason's Mill, Natal, and one in the Eastern Transvaal. These comprised two each of classes 1 and 1A. Up to November 1974 there were two class 1 and one class 1A, thereafter the last class 1 soldiered on at Glencoe until February 1975.

Preservation. No 1247 has been set aside for the National Railway Museum.

Industrial. A goodly number of these locomotives

A sturdy survivor of Hendrie's 1904 vintage 4–8–0s. Class 1A No 3 is seen at Apex Mines, Greenside Colliery, Blackhill, in 1976.

were sold to industry over many years, mainly before the currency of this book, although several were at work on various sites during the relevant period. It is probably most appropriate to restrict coverage to the four engines, three of which were at the time of writing entering their ninth decade of service.

SAR No	Builder	Works No	Date	Current owner and No
1252	North British	16377	1904	Randfontein Estates No 4
1277	North British	16402	1905	Apex Mines, Greenside No 2
1301	North British	19063	1909	Apex Mines, Greenside No 3
1443	North British	16417	1904	Gledhow Sugar Mill No 1 *Chaka*

The two Apex locomotives were overhauled during 1983–4 and are available as spares for the two ex-SAR 14Rs which normally perform. The Randfontein locomotive was also overhauled in 1983, exchanging blue for the new maroon livery, and was noted at work during August 1984. The Gledhow engine was being overhauled when seen in February 1985.

54

Class 3R 4–8–2 Ex-NGR Hendrie D class

It is almost pedantic to include this class, which disappeared so early during the period covered by this book. A direct development of the class 1A, these engines improved grate and ashpan conditions by placing the firebox behind the coupled wheels. As with the class 1A, plate frames were used, but a cast extension embraced the firebox. No superheater was fitted, but the slide valve cylinders were ½in larger diameter, just enough to propel the additional weight of the locomotive! Under SAR they became class 3, and in the Watson period were rebuilt with superheated standard boilers and became class 3R.

By the late 1960s the class was divided between the Orange Free State and Cape Western systems, entirely on shunting work, mainly at Bloemfontein, Cape Town, Touws River, and Beaufort West. By the time of this book, all active survivors were in the Cape Western system, the last survivors being laid-off in September 1973. Official stock figures, as at 1 April, were:

The World's first true 'Mountain' type locomotives, with wide firebox behind all coupled wheels, were Hendrie's class D for Natal in 1909. SAR No 1470, by then reboilered to class 3R, shunts at Noupoort 70 years later.

Year	1973	1974	1975	1976	1977
Active, Cape Western	9	–	–	–	–
Capital stock	23	9	8	7	–

Preservation. No 1474 was set aside for preservation, at De Aar. No 1453 was privately acquired by Clifford Harris, Wetton.
Industrial. Surprisingly, none of these locomotives was purchased for industrial service.
Number series. SAR 1446–75, ex-NGR 330–59. Built by North British 1909–10.

Class 3BR 4-8-2
Built new and rebuilt for SAR

Seen in 1975 at Landau 3 colliery, Blackhill, is a class 3BR as sold to industry – this example is in maroon livery.

The two-cylinder superheated 4-8-2 with piston valves and superheater was the most numerous basic type of locomotive used in South Africa. The Hendrie class 3B, as built with Belpaire firebox, was the pioneer of this particular breed, although its historical importance has rarely been properly recognised. Only ten were ordered, probably by the NGR, although delivered to the newly formed SAR in 1912. Mechanically, it was a superheated version of the class 3, with larger cylinders having piston valves, the running plate being raised to accommodate the increased height of these.

Only one had been withdrawn by April 1973, the remainder being at work on shunting duties in the Cape Western system. At the time they were being withdrawn the first World oil crisis had erupted, and the nine survivors were snapped-up by industrial users responding to the South African Government's call to save oil by using alternative sources of energy. Meanwhile, the SAR was replacing steam by diesels! Due to the fact that almost the whole class was sold, the decline of both active and capital stock totals kept pace remarkably closely.

Year, 1 April	1973	1974	1975	1976	1977
Active, Western Cape	9	7	–	–	–
Capital stock	10	10	8	1	–

Preservation. None was saved for preservation.
Industrial and number details.

SAR No	North British No	Buyer, new number
	(1912)	
1479	19597	Not sold
1480	19598	Vaal Reefs, Orkney No 4
1481	19599	Landau Colliery No 3
1482	19600	Western Holdings No 7, later Fregold North No 8
1483	19601	Blesbok Colliery No 3, later Springbok Colliery
1484	19688	Springbok Colliery Hope, Southern Cross steel, Umgala No 8
1485	19689	Free State Saaiplaas No 1
1486	19690	Western Holdings No 5, later to Umgala Colliery
1487	19691	Free State Geduld No 5, later Fregold North No 9
1488	19692	Vaal Reefs, Orkney No 5

Class 4AR 4–8–2
Built new for SAR

The class 4A and its rebuilds, class 4AR, exhibited several prophetic features. The gap in the running plate to allow easy access to piston valves was introduced in Germany about 40 years later. The rotary reversing shaft, ending in a compact gearbox above the expansion link, was 'invented' by British Railways for its standard locomotive classes!

One of the classics in locomotive evolution the Cape Government Railways only 4–8–2s which later became SAR class 4 combined the eight coupled wheels of the class 8 4–8–0 with the wide firebox over trailing truck of the 'Karoo' class Pacifics. Bar frames, outside cylinders, and inside Stephenson valve gear characterised all three types. So late in the day that they must have been ordered by SAR, perhaps due to an ex-CGR pressure group, the class 4A was a development with superheater, piston valves, and outside Walschaerts valve gear. Only ten were built for SAR, but a lighter version built simultaneously became the famous Rhodesian Railways 10th class, and totalled twenty. Anybody doubting the connection only needs to examine the chassis detailing, including the curious coupled wheel spacing common to SAR and RR.

Under SAR, the class 4A locomotives were rebuilt with Watson standard boilers and became class 4AR. Survivors of the class were stationed at Millsite shed, Krugersdorp, and by 1 April 1973 only

one was left, lasting until November 1973. In the capital stock lists there were six as at 31 March 1973, compared with only one a year later.

Preservation. No 1554 has been retained for the National Railway Museum.
Industrial.
Two 4ARs were sold into colliery service, both being found at Apex colliery, Greenside, as follows:
　　SAR 1557. Apex No 3, later renumbered 1. Withdrawn about 1983
　　SAR 1559. Apex No 4, withdrawn 1980.
Number series.
SAR 1551–60. Built by North British 1913.
Mythology.
A foreman at Krugersdorp (Millsite) shed once informed the author that before they were rebuilt, one of these engines was the fastest locomotive in the world! Clearly he was confusing a class 4A with an A4, but there seemed no purpose in correcting such a delightfully misheld illusion . . .!

Class 11 2–8–2 Ex-Central SAR

Despite its popularity elsewhere in the world, the 2–8–2 'Mikado' type never caught on in South Africa, and these locomotives, designed by Hyde, were the only SA Cape gauge class built in quantity. Very advanced for their time, they initially proved too heavy for the track, and some were stored until the track was upgraded. Built for heavy coal traffic from Witbank to Germiston, they were fairly rapidly ousted from this duty by other and larger types. Features included wide Belpaire fireboxes on boilers which were later superheated, and outside admission piston valves, driven by Walschaerts gear, giving a very free and modern sounding exhaust. So excellent were their features that 80 years after building, nearly half the class are still hard at work in industrial use, surely a world record.

In their later SAR days, most were used on shunting duties in the Cape Northern and Midland systems, and as at 1 April 1973 there were two on the CN and 18 on the CM. A year later, the CM was down to three examples, the class becoming extinct operationally during April 1975. Capital stock, as at 31 March, reduced as follows:

Year	1972	1973	1974	1975	1976	1977	1978
Stock	34	30	18	15	7	1	nil

Preservation. No 942 has been preserved outside Witbank station.

Industrial. Fifteen of the class have been sold, and sometimes resold, as below:

SAR No	Industrial user
918	President Brandt GM No 7
921	South Witbank Coal Mine, later Tavistock Colliery No 2
923	Western Holdings No 6
926	President Brandt GM No 6
928	President Steyn GM No 8
929	President Steyn GM No 6
932	President Brandt GM No 8
933	President Steyn GM No 7
936	ISCOR, Pretoria, No 18 or 19. Later Tavistock Colliery No 1, now withdrawn
938	President Brandt GM for spares
940	ISCOR, Pretoria, No 18 or 19. Later South Witbank Colliery No 6, currently Umgala Colliery, Utrecht, No 1
943	South Witbank Coal Mine, later Tavistock Colliery No 3. Now renumbered Tavistock 1
944	Free State Geduld GM No 6
945	Free State Saaiplaas GM No 2
946	Blue Circle Cement Co, Lichtenburg

Number series.
SAR 912–947, ex CSAR 700–35, built by North British, 1904.

Class 12R 4-8-2 Rebuilt from classes 12 and 12B

The class 12 built new for SAR, was the logical development of the Hendrie class 3B, and had the same features but enlarged throughout. The class 12B was almost identical, but had a slightly longer bogie wheelbase; they were built by Baldwin in America, plate frames and all! When rebuilt with Watson standard boilers, this minor difference was ignored, and in latter years all locomotives were class 12R.

During the relevant period they were allocated to three systems and used almost entirely on shunting duties. Those on the Cape Midland were stationed at Sydenham, Port Elizabeth, for shunting in the docks and in New Brighton marshalling yard, plus much trip working in the area. Right at the end, No 1505 was put into good fettle for an enthusiasts' special, and thereafter kept for such duties. Until the Uitenhage suburban trains were dieselised, it had a nice little job on a single out-and-back suburban run to Uitenhage.

Those in the Orange Free State were at Bloemfontein and Bethlehem, entirely for shunting, while the large contingent in the Western Transvaal were mainly at Germiston and Springs, plus one or two at Krugersdorp, again mainly for shunting. For several years one Germiston locomotive was kept in immaculate condition as passenger station pilot, and was a familiar sight to regular travellers.

The Springs locomotives were the most widely travelled, and were often used on local goods work on the branch to Nigel and Heidelberg, plus other trip workings in the East Rand area. Additionally, some were sub-shedded to Saaiwater and Vandyksdrift in the Witbank coalfield, and frequently ran along the electrified main line with short loads to and from the home shed at Springs, where washouts took place. It was in 1974, when Hendrina power station experienced some sort of failure in the middle of midwinter peak demand, that coal had to be urgently transferred from Hendrina to other power stations, using the shunters from Vandyksdrift. At the time these were classes 12R, 12A and 12AR, which for their last time engaged in the coal haulage for which they were designed.

In 1980, during a peak in Zambia's perpetual motive power crisis, ten 12Rs were hired to ZR (see Chapter 4), but were soon returned to SAR. Surprisingly few 12Rs found their way into industrial service, despite their evident suitability, this being largely a matter of becoming available at times when the industrial market was already saturated with other often less suitable locomotives.

Distribution and capital stock of the class was as below.

Preservation. At present, No 1505 locomotive has been put aside for preservation.

Industrial. The following 12Rs have been sold into industrial service:

SAR	Industrial user
1510	Umgala Colliery, Utrecht No 7
1511	Middelplaas Manganese SL001
1515	Tweefontein Colliery, later to Witbank Consolidated Coal Mines
1863	Middelplaas Manganese SL002
1865	Middelplaas Manganese SL003
1936	Enyati Colliery, later Western Holdings GM No 8

Number series.
1494–1501 North British 1912
1502–1509 North British 1913
1510–1519 North British 1915
1859–1878 Beyer Peacock 1922
1931–1960 Baldwin 1920 (ex-class 12B).

Year	1973	1974	1975	1976	1977	1978	1979	1980	1981	1982	1983	1984	1985	1986	1987	1988
Capital	74	74	74	74	73	73*	73*	73	72	70	70	8	3	1	1	1
Operating																
Cape Midland	21	25	25	25	25	26	26	26	26	1	1	1	1	1	1	1
Orange Free State	19	4	4	4	–	–	–	–	–	–	–	–	–	–	–	–
West Transvaal	34	44	44	44	48	47	47	34	43	5	–	–	–	–	–	–
Active SAR	74	73	73	73	73	73	73	60	69	6	1	1	1	1	1	1
Staged SAR	–	–	–	–	–	1	1	1	1	63	67	5	5	5	40	13
Hired to Zambia	–	–	–	–	–	–	–	10	–	–	–	–	–	–	–	–
Total	74	73	73	73	73	74*	74*	71	70	69	68	6	6	6	41	14

*Official figures disagree.

(top left)
An immaculate class 11 of Tavistock Colliery shows little signs of 70 years' hard service as it shunts coal trucks at the mine.

(below left)
For some reason few class 12R locomotives were sold to industry, for which they seemed eminently suitable. No 1515 is depicted at Tweefontein Colliery in 1982.

Classes 12A and 12AR 4–8–2 Built new and rebuilt for SAR

Although very different in appearance, it is impossible to consider these two classes separately as they differed only in their boiler design, and tended often to be allocated irrespectively of this. All were built as class 12A, and the class 12AR were reboilerings from class 12A. As may be expected from the class number, they were developed from class 12, and were considerably enlarged all round, other than wheel diameter. Apart from sheer enlargement, the Belpaire fireboxes, common to both classes, were extended in the 12A to include a combustion chamber. At the front end, the class 12 cylinders had small steam chests and indirect 'Z' ports, while the class 12A had much more direct ports and therefore larger steam chests. With these more modern cylinders the sound of a class 12A locomotive, really opened up, was quite impressive.

The class 12AR reboilerings used a boiler designed by Dr M. M. Loubser, the then CME. Loubser was apparently very much a workshop man, with initial and repair costs uppermost in his mind, and the 12AR boilers, lacking combustion chambers, were considered by engine crews to be inferior steamers. The lay observer usually reckons the 12AR to have 'a much larger boiler' than the 12A, but this is not so. What happened was that the rebuilt engines had much higher-pitched boilers to increase firebox depth, and partly nullify the reduction in volume due to elimination of the combustion chamber. The actual boiler diameter was almost the same, but shorter chimneys and domes gave the bigger look. A shortened 12AR boiler was later used on the new class S1 shunting engines.

The unrebuilt engines were, at the start of this survey, mostly in the Western Transvaal, divided between Springs and Germiston. One was at De Aar in the Cape Northern, and a few in the Eastern Transvaal at Nelspruit and Waterval Boven. All were used mainly on shunting, but the Springs engines were also used on the same line duties as recorded for class 12R. Quite suddenly in 1977 all the 12A were concentrated on the Cape Northern where they shunted at De Aar, a few occasionally being moved to Beaconsfield, Kimberley.

The more numerous rebuilt engines were more widely distributed, those on the Cape Northern being at De Aar and Kimberley for shunting. Two on the Cape Eastern were at East London, again mainly for shunting, but were also observed on suburban passenger and local freight duties. The Orange Free State engines were at Kroonstad for shunting. All the Natal allocation were at Glencoe, and were 'leftovers' from engines which hauled coal between there and Vryheid in pre-electrification

days. After electrification, they replaced older power on the Glencoe shunts, and worked the Burnside branch, while a couple were sub-shedded at Newcastle for the shunt and if rumour is right, the odd trip to Utrecht.

Eastern Transvaal 12ARs were mainly at Nelspruit and Waterval Boven for shunting, but could sometimes appear in the Witbank area. On the Western Transvaal, Germiston and Springs claimed the class with much the same division of duties as mentioned for classes 12R and 12A, except that for several years all have been at Germiston, and especially at its sub-shed of Kazerne, in south-east Johannesburg. As of 1983, class 12AR locomotives could be seen as far out as the Kempton Park shunt-cum-pickup, but at September 1984, the most likely venue was Kazerne yard. By the time this book is published, the class will probably be extinct.

Preservation. 12A 2111 has been retained for the National Railway Museum and is being restored to working order. 12AR 1535 is similarly retained but in working order for special trains. 2111 is being restored to working order in 1989.

Industrial. No ex-SAR/SATS locomotives have been sold into industrial service, but eight class 12A, outwardly similar to the SAR locomotives although devoid of superheaters, were built new for industrial service by North British from 1947 to 1953. Most of these remain in service.

Number series.

Class 12A	Rebuilt to 12AR
1520–29 North British 1920	1520/22/23/29
1530–50 Henschel 1928–9	1530/32/34/35/36/37/ 40–46/49/50
2103–10 Henschel 1929	2103/04/05/08/09/10
2111–25 North British 1921	2112/13/15/16/18–22/ 24/25
2126–38 North British 1929	2127/28/29/31/35/36/37

(top right) *The last duties of SAR's handsome Belpaire boiler class 12A locomotives was shunting at De Aar, to which depot all were transferred. Here No 1539, in clean condition, shunts at the main marshalling yard in 1982.*

(below right) *Class 12AR No 2103 displays its massive bulk in the yard at Springs shed in 1979.*

60

Capital stock at 31 March

Class	1973	1974	1975	1976	1977	1978	1979	1980	1981	1982	1983	1984	1985	1986	1987	1988
12A	23	23	23	23	23	23	23	23	23	23	23	1	–	–	–	–
12AR	44	44	44	44	44	44	44	44	44	44	44	24	14	1	1	1

Class 12A operating stock at 1 April

Year	1973	1974	1975	1976	1977	1978	1979	1980	1981	1982	1983	1984	1985	1986	1987	1988
Cape Northern	1	1	1	1	1	23	23	23	23	14	13	–	–	–	–	–
West Transvaal	17	20	20	20	21*	–	–	–	–	–	–	–	–	–	–	–
East Transvaal	5	2	2	2	3*	–	–	–	–	–	–	–	–	–	–	–
Staged	–	–	–	–	–	–	–	–	–	9	9	1	1	1	22	1
Totals	23	23	23	23	25*	23	23	23	23	23	22	1	1	1	22	1

*Official figures incorrect.

Class 12AR operating stock at 1 April

Year	1973	1974	1975	1976	1977	1978	1979	1980	1981	1982	1983	1984	1985	1986	1987	1988
Cape Northern	13	18	18	18	18	11	9	9	9	9	16	–	–	–	–	–
Cape Eastern	2	2	2	2	2	–	–	–	–	–	–	–	–	–	–	–
Orange Free State	5	–	–	–	–	–	–	–	–	–	–	–	–	–	–	–
Natal	8	8	8	8	8	8	8	8	8	8	–	–	–	–	–	–
West Transvaal	12	12	12	12	11*	19	26	27	27	27	23	17	1	1	1	1
East Transvaal	4	4	4	4	3*	6	1	–	–	–	–	–	–	–	–	–
Active	44	44	44	44	42*	44	44	44	44	44	39	17	1	1	1	1
Staged	–	–	–	–	–	–	–	–	–	–	5	7	26	26	36	2
Totals	44	44	44	44	42*	44	44	44	44	44	44	24	27	27	37	3

*Official figures incorrect.

A class 12A unrebuilt Hendrie 4–8–2 leaves Broodsnyersplaas with coal empties for Hendrina power station, along what became eventually the Richard's Bay coal line. Christine Durrant

Class 14R 4–8–2 Built new and rebuilt for SAR

Class 14R No 1911 at De Aar damaged its tender in a minor collision, and was paired rather attractively with a class 24 tender until it was withdrawn.

The 14th series of classes date back to the days when it was imagined that small differences in wheel diameter had disproportionate effects on performance. Hendrie already had his 3ft 9in wheel class 3B and his 4ft 3in class 12, but for the steeply-graded lines in Natal the intermediate 14 class with 4ft 0in wheels was evolved. Apart from these differences in wheel diameters, the 14 class was better than either, having more modern cylinder design with straighter ports and larger steam chest volume than the earlier classes, the first Hendrie design with these features.

Three versions of the original design were built, firstly the 45 original 14 class with 16·2-ton axle load. Forty-one were built as class 14A, with 6in less boiler diameter, to bring axle loading down to 15 tons for lighter track. Finally there were fifteen of class 14B which was an unsuperheated 14, the theory being that with frequent stops as on the old Natal main line a superheater was not necessary. This was rapidly disproved, and superheaters fitted.

Apart from No 1750 sold out of service before rebuilding, all were rebuilt with standard Watson boilers, becoming uniformly class 14R in the process. In the years relevant to this book, a small contingent was in the Cape Northern system, one at De Aar and the remainder at Klerksdorp for shunting. The majority were in Natal before dieselisation and electrification, distributed widely around the system and used mainly for shunting, although getting in some line work, especially on the North coast line. As late as 1975, two were noted double-heading a northbound passenger train, deputising for the usual GMAM. The last were at Mason's Mill, Pietermaritzburg.

As they were displaced from Natal, many moved to the Western Transvaal, mainly to Krugersdorp and Volksrust, where they were again employed on shunting, but have now been displaced by larger locomotives and diesels.

Sprightly and generally useful locomotives, they have been welcome outside South Africa, and after the collapse of Moçambique's motive power, were the mainstay of the Swaziland Railway until later replaced by 15ARs. Similarly, while Zimbabwe was rebuilding its Garratt fleet, SAR Garratts were first hired but not found fully suitable. After that, 14Rs were hired for shunting, releasing indigenous Garratts for main line work. These have now been returned, after being the last non-Garratt steam to see regular service on the National Railways of Zimbabwe.

Capital stock, and distribution in service are tabulated below:

Year	1973	1974	1975	1976	1977	1978	1979	1980	1981	1982	1983	1984	1985	1986	1987	1988
Capital (31 March)	99	99	99	99	98	98	98	98	85	84	84	6	2	4	11	–
Operating (1 April)																
Cape Northern	15	15	15	15	15	15	15	15	12	1	1	–	–	–	–	–
Natal	84	84	83	46	43	22	14	13	13	2	1	–	–	–	–	–
West Transvaal	–	–	–	37	40	47	52	42	38	16	1	–	–	–	–	–
Active SAR	99	99	98	98	98	84	81	80	63	19	3	–	–	–	–	–
Staged SAR	–	–	–	–	–	–	–	–	–*	58*	69	4	–	4	11	–
Hired Zimbabwe	–	–	–	–	–	–	–	–	6	14	–	–	–	–	–	–
Hired Swaziland	–	–	–	–	–	14	16	15	12	3	1	–	–	–	–	–
Totals	99	99	98	98	98	98	97	95	81*	94*	73	4	2	4	11	–

*The 1981 total appears to omit staged locomotives, later included in 1982.

Preservation. Four 14R have been preserved, No 1576 at the Umgeni Steam Railway, Gledhow; No 1718 at Midmar, Natal; No 1733 for the National Railway Museum and No 1909 to the RSSA Collection, Krugersdorp.

Industrial. Numerous 14Rs have been sold into industrial service, as below:

SAR No	Industrial user
1586	Rustenburg Platinum Mines No 1586
1589	Vaal Reefs GM *Bob*
1701	Apex Colliery, Greenside No 5
1705	Grootvlei Proprietory Mines Ltd No 5 *Joyce*
1711	Rustenburg Platinum Mines No 1711
1714	Rustenburg Platinum Mines No 1714 (Also carried No 5 plates, now removed)
1719	Rustenburg Platinum Mines No 1719
1723	Natal Cambrian Colliery, Ballangeiech
1729	Vaal Reefs GM
1730	Randfontein Estates GM No 5
1732	Rustenburg Platinum Mines No 1732
1735	Rustenburg Platinum Mines No 1735
1737	Grootvlei Proprietory Mines Ltd No 4, later No 6 *Graham*

SAR No	Industrial user
1740	Newcastle Platberg Colliery, later Ballangeiech Colliery, scrapped
1745	Natal Cambrian Colliery, Ballangeich, No 2
1750	Unrebuilt locomotive to ISCOR No 15, later Enyati Colliery No 3
1754	Rustenburg Platinum Mines No 1754
1755	St Helena Gold Mines No 7
1757	Grootvlei Proprietory Mines Ltd
1759	Rustenburg Platinum Mines No 1759
1906	Randfontein Estates GM No 6
1908	Apex Colliery, Greenside No 4
1918	St Helena Gold Mines
1921	Grootvlei Proprietory Mines Ltd No 3 *Duggie*

Number series.

1701–20 Robert Stephenson & Co 1913–14. Originally class 14

1721–45 Robert Stephenson & Co 1915. Originally class 14

1576–95 North British 1914. Originally class 14A

1901–21 North British 1915. Originally class 14A

1746–60 Beyer Peacock 1915. Originally class 14B

ABOVE: Randfontein Estates Gold Mines No 4 *Trixie*, ex-SAR class 1A, and built for the Natal Government Railway, draws ore hoppers through Millsite plant in the 1970s. This locomotive has now been re-painted maroon.

LEFT: Grootvlei Proprietory Mine No 3 *Puffing Duggie*, ex-SAR class 8DW and originally Cape Government Railways, hauls ore hoppers towards the plant in 1982. This locomotive has now been withdrawn from service.

ABOVE: Landau Colliery's class 3BR in dark maroon livery hauls coal towards SAR's interchange sidings at Blackhill in the late 1970s.

LEFT: President Brand's ex-SAR, and originally CSAR class 11 2–8–2s are probably in better condition than when first out-shopped by North British in Glasgow, over 80 years ago!

RIGHT: The 'fully dieselised' main line from East London saw several regular steam workings over various sections, of which the most spectacular was the Queenstown–Burgersdorp line. Climbing Bosmanshoek Pass with the daily local freight are a domeless 19D plus 15AR combination, seen late afternoon when the light was at its very best.

TOP LEFT: On the line from Hendrina to Vandyksdrift a class 12AR locomotive trundles loaded coal hoppers across the barren wastes near the power station.

LEFT: A 15BR, sold to Randfontein Estates Gold Mines, approaches Millsite with a mineworkers' train in the mid-1970s.

ABOVE: The last two 14CRBs to leave East London on transfer to Cape Town double-headed a light freight to Queenstown before continuing their journey light engine. (*Photo P. A. Stow*)

TOP LEFT: Several experimental liveries were used on Rustenburg Platinum Mines during the early 1980s. Unfortunately, lack of cleanliness spoilt the effects, and black was eventually restored. Here a splendid maroon 14R heads ore to the plant in 1981. Another 14R was in Brunswick green. (*Photo the late J. B. Cornish*)

LEFT: RPM also tried out blue on one of its class 15CB, both light and dark blues being used. Here, the light blue version is reflected in the still waters of the Hex River as it heads towards the plant with loads of ore. (*Photo the late J. B. Cornish*)

ABOVE: On the Underberg branch, a diminutive GCA is silhouetted against golden fields, while the distant Drakensberg mountain range is capped with snow.

The Groot Swartberg range frowns down on the fertile valley where a clean Oudshoorn class 19D provides smoke and steam to complement visibly the cocks that are still crowing in the early morning.

TOP LEFT: The Piketberg range near Het Kruis looms behind a poppet-valve 19C heading north on the Bitterfontein branch, shortly before dieselisation.

LEFT: The daily passenger train from Pieterburg winds round an S-bend between Duiwelskloof and Tzaneen in the mid-1970s. Motive power is one of Pietersburg's well kept 15F class.

ABOVE: Realising the tourist potential of steam power, SAR is now running regularly scheduled steam specials between George and Knysna, in peak holiday times, using the class 24 locomotives normally employed on the branch. Easter 1984 saw one of these trains near Goukamma, in a colourful and scenic setting.

RIGHT: New Year 1973 sees a pair of class 25 condensing 4–8–4s rolling through the rugged Karoo near Biesiespoort with a block grain train bound for Cape Town.

ABOVE: On long weekends, the 07.45 Bethlehem to Ficksburg was often double-headed, with long trains conveying Sotho workers returning to Lesotho (formerly Basutoland) from Johannesburg. Here the return train accelerates out of Generalsnek headed by a pair of class 25NC 4–8–4s.

RIGHT: The scale of mountain railway operation in South Africa is typified by the manner in which a large GEA Garratt is dwarfed by the looming terrain as the locomotive negotiates Houw Hoek pass with the Caledon to Belleville freight, in 1975.

When Randfontein Estates Gold Mines greatly expanded their operations around 1980 onwards, diesels, electrics, road haulage, and conveyor belts were all investigated and found much more expensive than a straight railway using coal-burning steam. To haul the required loads, surplus SAR class GMAM Garratts were bought, and initially painted in the old mine livery of blue. No R10, the last blue Garratt, is seen easing orange hoppers out of Cooke 2 shaft in 1984.

RIGHT: Even though SAR's new Blue Train has never been steam-hauled in regular revenue service, Capital Park shed saw to it that the short empty stock shunt in Pretoria had a blue locomotive. Originally there was a blue S2, later replaced by a 19D of similar hue, which was still in operation in April 1985. An early shot of the locomotive with short tender shows the train leaving the Blue Train shed in the mid-1970s.

BELOW RIGHT: Vryheid Coronation Colliery, Natal, originally painted its locomotives blue. In the early 1980s green was selected, resulting in a class GEA in that colour on empty hoppers for the Vrede section, about 1982.

BELOW: Nice though the blue livery was, mine management later decided on an even more handsome maroon, with black-and-gold trim, to which all new acquisitions and most older locomotives now conform. GMAM No R17, suitably resplendent, is seen en route to Millsite plant, also in 1984.

ABOVE: Rhodesian locomotive crews *like* Garratts, and such SAR favourites as classes 15E, 15F and 19D have fared poorly north of the Limpopo. The six class 15Fs hired to RR were restricted to the Bulawayo–Gwelo line, and seen, typically, on the passenger train near Heany junction. (*Photo C. E. Rickwood*)

BELOW: Wardale's rebuilt class 19D No 2644 departs from Mareetsane with the southbound Mafikeng–Vryburg passenger train, on a July morning.

Classes 14CR, 14CRB, and 14CRM 4–8–2 Built new and rebuilt by SAR

These externally indistinguishable locomotives were Canadian-built versions of class 14, and were ordered at a time when motive power was desperately needed, yet unobtainable from the traditional British sources. Since the Canadians (unlike Baldwin) were not prepared to try their hands at British type plate frames, American bar frames were included, together with cylinders cast with half-saddles. This was by no means a new departure for SAR, many of the old CGR types such as class 8 being of similar construction. With the new locomotives came an even better cylinder design than in the 14 class, with larger and straighter ports giving a very sharp, free, exhaust. The first 60 locomotives were considerably lighter than the final 13, which had heavy weights attached to the frames to increase adhesion. In time, most of the earlier locomotives had their weight redistributed to reduce the axle load and adhesion weight, by increasing the loads on leading bogie and trailing truck, rather misleadingly referred to as rebalancing. The unmodified locomotives remained class 14C, the rebalanced engines class 14CB (B for branch lines), and the heavy version 14CM (M for main lines). In due course all were reboilered with Watson standard boilers, becoming classes 14CR, 14CRB, and 14CRM respectively.

In their long lives they have been used widely over the SAR, but during the currency of this book, have been mainly in two systems. On the Cape Western they have been stationed mainly at Paarden Eiland shed, Cape Town, at first largely on local goods services, but latterly mainly on dock and other shunting. They also appeared at other sheds in the system, such as Beaufort West, also for shunting. A solitary locomotive represented the class at De Aar on the Cape Northern system.

Earlier, many were on the Cape Eastern, stationed at East London, these being the remnants of a larger allocation which formerly worked to Umtata and Cookhouse. During 1973–78, apart from shunting, they worked pick-up freights to Amabele on the main line, and participated in East London suburban workings. The last two at East London, when leaving for Cape Town, double-headed a freight as far as Queenstown, the first steam train on this section for many years.

Those in the Eastern Transvaal were the survivors of a larger allocation divided between Witbank and Pietersburg, and engaged mainly on shunting,

Class 14 CRM No 2033 poses among much larger class 15F and class 25 condenser locomotives at Beaufort West shed.

although the Witbank locomotives were also used on the Stoffberg line until larger power became available. Details of capital and operating stock are listed below:

Across the Atlantic. On the right is British-built class 14R with plate frames and low running plate, while on the left is the North American version class 14CRM with bar frames and high running plate. Details also differ in motion components.

Year	1973	1974	1975	1976	1977	1978	1979	1980	1981	1982	1983	1984	1985	1986	1987	1988
Capital (31 March)	70	70	70	68	68	67	67	67	65	62	51	4	4	4	2	–
Operating (1 April)																
Cape Western	41	41	44	42	45	59	65	64	63	3	–	–	–	–	–	–
Cape Northern	–	–	–	–	1	1	1	1	1	–	–	–	–	–	–	–
Cape Eastern	26	25	25	25	21	7	–	–	–	–	–	–	–	–	–	–
East Transvaal	3	3	–	–	–	–	–	–	–	–	–	–	–	–	–	–
Active	70	69	69	67	67	67	66	65	64	3	–	–	–	–	–	–
Staged	–	–	–	–	1	1	–	1	1	49	47	5	4	4	2	–
Total	70	69	69	67	68	68	66	66	65	52	47	5	4	4	2	–

Preservation. Four 14CRB have been preserved; No 1761 for RSSA Cape Town; No 1764 at Oude Meester distillery, Stellenbosch; No 1882 for the National Railway Museum, and No 2010 at Ashton.
Industrial. Although very suitable for industrial use, none has been purchased due to the high cost of haulage from Cape Town to the industrial areas.

International. A slightly lighter version of the original 14C was produced by the same builders in 1918 and 1921, as Rhodesian Railways class 11. In 1948 a further batch was built as RR class 11A.

Some of the 11s and all the 11A were sold to Moçambique, from whence they operated into Swaziland.

Number series and builder	Variations
1761–80 Built Montreal 1918	1762–64 class 14CR, others 14CRB
1881–1900 Built Montreal 1919	1894/98 class 14CR, others 14CRB
1991–2010 Built Montreal 1919	All 14CRB
2026–38 Built Montreal 1922	2035 class 14CR, others 14CRM

Classes 15A and 15AR 4-8-2 Built new and rebuilt by SAR

These mixed-traffic locomotives were the final development of the Hendrie plate-framed 4–8–2s, being not only his most useful but his most numerous group of motive power. Development was in four major stages, the first of which comprised the ten locomotives class 15, having Belpaire fireboxes without combustion chambers. These were developed into class 15A, with combustion chambers, and fifteen were built retaining the narrow cab and dropped running plate at the rear end, as with the 15 class. The final Hendrie style incorporated at the rear end a straight running plate supporting a wider cab. Finally, all the 15 and most of the 15A class were re-fitted with Watson standard boilers, becoming uniformly class 15AR. During the currency of this book, there remained in service two 15A, No 1791 of the narrow cab version, stationed at Capital Park, Pretoria, and doing little other than special work, while No 1970 *Millie* was famous at De Aar as the station pilot.

The 15AR class locomotives showed their true mixed-traffic status by being stationed widely throughout the railway, and used on everything from dock shunting to main line passenger work. During the currency of this book they have been allocated to five SAR systems, and hired to one other country, some 90 per cent of the class still being in existence at the end of 1983, seventy-four of them nominally active.

The Cape Northern examples were scattered between De Aar, Kimberley, and Klerksdorp, mainly on shunting duties, but the Cape Midland steadily became a major user of the class. Most of the CM allocation has been at Sydenham where at first they hauled main line trains out to Klipplaat, where others were stationed for continuing to Graaf

For many years the last unrebuilt class 15A locomotive has been De Aar's famous station pilot, No 1970 Milly, *displaying her elegant Edwardian figure!*

Reinet. They also handled the tightly-timed suburban services from Port Elizabeth to Uitenhage until these were dieselised in 1982. As the main line services were placed in the hands of Garratts, the 15ARs drifted into shunting and trip working at Port Elizabeth, while nine examples handle the shunting at Midlandia, Noupoort.

The Cape Eastern system was largely dieselised along its main line, but retained many steam worked branches until 1982–83. Some of these are really secondary main lines, with steam worked trains hauled by the veteran 15ARs until 1983. The allocations were at East London itself, where they performed shunting and suburban work until 1976, including the daily passenger train to Kingwilliamstown. East London shed closed in 1984. A large allocation was based on Queenstown, many being sub-shedded at Burgersdorp for the line to Rosmead. Right up to 1982, the East London to Cape Town passenger trains could be experienced on this line with single- or double-headed 15ARs, very good work for 60-year-old engines. They also operated from Burgersdorp to Aliwal North, and working to and from Queenstown main shed for washouts, hauled the pick-up goods along the main line, including the famous Bosmanshoek pass.

The Western Transvaal locomotives were mainly active at Springs on local freight and shunting work, which latter duty also saw the class at Germiston and Volksrust. In the Eastern Transvaal, they were to be found at Pretoria and Witbank, including working between these places, at Breyten, where

The last built class 15A was No 2100, originally fitted with Lentz poppet valves. Here, as class 15AR in 1979, with standard cylinders and Watson standard boiler, it shows no signs of its original experimental condition. Photographed at Burgersdorp coaling stage.

they worked local traffic to Piet Retief, and on shunting at all these places, plus Nelspruit and Waterval Boven.

Currently, the only place to see 15ARs on any-thing but shunting is in Swaziland, where they took over duties from the 14Rs, and are in turn due for replacement by diesels.

Distribution and stock totals are tabulated below:

Year	1973	1974	1975	1976	1977	1978	1979	1980	1981	1982	1983	1984	1985	1986	1987	1988
Capital *(31 March)*																
15A	2	2	2	2	2	2	2	2	2	2	2	1	1	1	–	–
15AR	118	118	118	118	116	116	116	116	115	115	115	84	72	63	57	42
Operating *(1 April, class 15AR)*																
Cape Northern	11	6	–	–	–	–	–	–	–	–	–	–	–	–	–	–
Cape Midland	27	41	44	44	44	44	70	70	70	55	49	43	63	55	51	39
Cape Eastern	24	29	35	35	39	55	46	46	45	45	33	11	9	8	6	3
West Transvaal	19	19	18	21	21	12	–	–	–	–	–	–	–	–	–	–
East Transvaal	37	23	20	16	12	5	–	–	–	–	–	–	–	–	–	–
Active SAR	118	118	117	116	116	116	116	116	115	100	82	55	72	63	57	42
Staged SAR	–	–	–	–	–	–	–	–	–	–	13	16	16	22	41	39
Hired Swaziland	–	–	–	–	–	–	–	–	–	15	17	20	21	19	10	8
Totals	118	118	117	116	116	116	116	116	115	115	112	90	109	104	108	89

Preservation. Two 15A, No 1791 and No 1970, have been retained for the National Railway Museum. Of the 15AR, No 1850 has been similarly reserved, No 1963 bought by the Umgeni Steam Railway, and No 2016 preserved at Queenstown.

Industrial. None has yet been sold into industry.

Number series	SAR No	Builder	Date	Type	Later types
	1561–70	North British	1914	15	All 15AR
	1571–75	North British	1914	15A (narrow cab)	All 15AR
	1781–88	North British	1914–5	15A (narrow cab)	All 15AR
	1789–98	North British	1915	15A (narrow cab)	15AR except No 1791*
	1799–1804	North British	1916	15A (narrow cab)	All 15AR
	1805–08	North British	1917	15A (narrow cab)	All 15AR
	1809–28	North British	1920	15A (wide cab)	15AR except No 1824*
	1839–58	Beyer Peacock	1920	15A (wide cab)	15AR except Nos 1845 & 1851
	1961–70	Beyer Peacock	1921	15A (wide cab)	15AR except No 1970
	2011–25	North British	1921	15A (wide cab)	All 15AR
	2080–2100	Maffei	1925	15A (wide cab)	All 15AR

*One other class 15A was not rebuilt, either No 1790, No 1794, or No 1812.

Class 15BR 4–8–2 Built new and rebuilt by SAR

These 30 locomotives, like the class 14C, were supplied from Canada at a time when European builders could not cope with new orders. Dimensionally they resembled the class 15A, but in transatlantic detail were more akin to the smaller-wheeled 14Cs. Built as class 15B, all had been rebuilt with Watson standard boilers and reclassified 15BR.

By the currency of this book, all were in the Cape Western system, mainly at Paarden Eiland shed, Cape Town, where they worked local goods and passenger trains to Malmesbury, and freight to Sir Lowry's Pass, plus the inevitable shunting. A few were at Worcester for shunting, with one sub-shedded at Ashton for the same duty. The normal way of exchanging the Ashton shunter once fortnightly was to use it on the local passenger train, otherwise Garratt hauled.

Capital and operational stock totals were:

A lean and lanky class 15BR glints in the late afternoon sun at Tweefontein Colliery's new 1980 locomotive shed. Additional handrails have been added for mine service.

International. Twelve 15BR were sold to the CFM (Moçambique Railways) in 1973, in two batches. The relevant renumberings SAR/CFM are as given to the author by the Chief Mechanical Engineer of CFM, but there is some doubt as to whether they are correct. There is now no way of confirming the CFM renumbering. For what it is worth, the official version is:

Loco No	March 1973 batch	Loco No	July 1973 batch
SAR	CFM	SAR	CFM
1836	421	1829	427
1974	426	1831	428
1981	422	1838	429
1983	423	1976	430
1984	424	1977	431
1986	425	1985	432

Year	1973	1974	1975	1976	1977	1978	1979	1980	1981	1982	1983
Capital	29	16	12	9	4	2	2	1	1	1	–
Operational Cape Western	27	12	4	3	–	–	–	–	–	–	–

Preservation. No 1979 has been retained for the National Railway Museum.

Industrial. Six were sold into industrial use:

SAR No	Industrial user
1972	Tweefontein United Collieries No 5
1973	Randfontein Estates GM No 2, scrapped December 1983
1975	Randfontein Estates GM, second No 2
1980	Tweefontein United Collieries No 4
1982	Randfontein Estates GM No 3
1990	Randfontein Estates GM No 1, scrapped

In Moçambique they were mainly used for shunting at Lourenço Marques (now Maputo), and occasionally ran to Swaziland.

Number series.

1829–38	Built Montreal	1918
1971–90	Built Montreal	1922

Class 15CA 4–8–2 Built new for SAR

The 15CA was a direct development of the 15CB, the 'A' suffix designating Alco, which built the first batch. In most major details and dimensions the locomotives were identical to the CB version, except for the rear framing. Whereas the CBs had straight-through bar frames from buffer beam to drag box, the CAs reverted to something akin to the Hendrie arrangement, with a cast cradle connecting the main frames to the wide-spaced sub-frames embracing the ashpan. Theoretically it gave more ashpan space, but later locomotives with larger grates reverted to the straight-through frame arrangement.

During their long lives, the 15CAs have been allocated everywhere from Cape Town to the Northern Transvaal, with the exception of the Cape Eastern and Midland systems. The class remained intact until 1973, since when only a handful have been withdrawn. From 1973 to 1978 all were in the Eastern Transvaal, stationed mainly at Pretoria and Witbank, between which they worked the main

Class 15CA No 2850, once Pretoria's crack passenger locomotive, pauses at Cullinan in 1980 prior to taking the Saturday afternoon local train to the Hoofstad *(Capital).*

line until electrification. After that, most remained at those two centres, replacing older engines on shunting duties, for which they are very popular being powerful, sure-footed, and low on maintenance. Other sheds in the Eastern Transvaal system were Pietersburg, which used them on main line work to Tzaneen and Messina, and Breyten which had a few for heavy shunting. A passenger duty they retained until the end of the service in 1983 were the local trains between Pretoria and Cullinan, which they performed with great vigour.

After 1978, when the Koedoespoort works closed to steam repairs, their overhauls wer transferred to Pietermaritzburg, which was also given an allocation of them for shunting, these remaining until Natal lost its remaining 3ft 6in steam in 1983. The Natal 15CAs went to the Cape Northern system for shunting to Mafikeng, Beaconsfield and De Aar, this system building-up to a maximum of 26 locomotives in September 1983. However, at Mafikeng they were found too heavy for the track, and dispersed to the Transvaal. From April 1984, the Eastern and Western Transvaal systems were renamed Northern and Southern Transvaal respectively, a geographically more logical nomenclature originally suggested by the author twelve years earlier, in *Steam on the Veld*. The Western/Southern Transvaal started to receive 15CAs in March 1983, and have now built up to 39 of the class stationed at Germiston and Kaserne, where they have replaced 12ARs and S1 classes. It is expected that they will remain on heavy shunting duties virtually to the end of steam.

Distribution of the class annually as at 31 March was as follows:

Year	1973	1974	1975	1976	1977	1978	1979	1980	1981	1982	1983	1984	1985	1986	1987	1988
Cape Northern	–	–	–	–	–	–	–	–	–	–	–	20	11	5	5	7
Natal	–	–	–	–	–	–	13	13	13	13	10	–	–	–	–	–
West Transvaal	–	–	–	–	–	–	–	–	–	–	11	27	39	42	31	15
East Transvaal	84	82	81	81	80	80	67	67	66	66	50	26	26	28	27	22
Working	84	82	81	81	80	80	80	80	79	79	71	73	76	75	63	44
Staged	–	–	–	–	–	–	–	–	–	–	7	4	–	1	11	18
Totals	84	82	81	81	80	80	80	80	79	79	78	77	76	76	74	62

Preservation. No 2055 has been preserved outside Rustenburg station and No 2850 has been reserved for the National Railway Museum.
Industrial. No 2807 and No 2839 have been sold to Rustenburg Platinum Mines, via Dunn's.

Number series.

SAR Nos	Builder	Date
2039–59	Alco	1926
2072–73	Alco	1926
2074–77	Baldwin	1929
2801–10	Breda	1929
2811–39	North British	1929
2840–57	North British	1930

Class 15CB 4–8–2 Built new for SAR

The class 15C locomotives were the prototypes of large modern steam power on SAR, and resulted from a visit by an official to the USA to study American motive power and to ascertain its suitability for South African conditions. Four prototypes were initially ordered, two class 15C mixed-traffic locomotives, known as 'Big Bills', and two class 16D Pacifics for passenger work, the 'Big Berthas'. Their immediate success led to further orders, some to modified designs, such that the initial 4–8–2 became class 15CB, the B supposedly standing for Baldwin.

They were very much the big American engine scaled down to Cape gauge size, which gauge for gauge is almost three-quarters of standard gauge. Originally South Africa's top-link engines, they were gradually downgraded to local goods and shunting, but always on heavy work where they thrived. In 1973 the four stationed in the Eastern Transvaal were at Witbank, and sub-shedded at Derwent for working the Roossenekal ore branch. The remainder were on the Western Transvaal at Krugersdorp for heavy shunting and trip working. Early in 1976 they were transferred to Springs, nominally for 'storage', but being too good to sit idle the Springs foreman used them for shunting, not only in Springs yard but down in the coalfields at Saaiwater and Vandyksdrift. The story is told that some had to be hastily recalled from these sub-sheds when potential buyers wanted to examine the locomotives 'stored' at Springs.

There is hardly need to tabulate their allocation, as at 1 April 1973 there were four in the Eastern

Class 15CB No 2070, as South Witbank Coal Mine No 1, sits at the mine's locomotive depot in 1969, soon after purchase from SAR.

Transvaal system and eight in the Western. By April 1974 all were Western Transvaal, remaining until August 1976 when the prototype was retained for preservation and the remainder sold. At the time of writing, the class is 58–59 years old, and every locomotive is in existence, eleven out of twelve still at work!

Preservation. No 2060 retained by SAR for preservation.

Industrial. Eleven were sold to industry, all of which remain at work.

SAR No	Industrial user
2061	South Witbank Coal Mine No 3
2062	Tweefontein United Collieries
2063	Dunn's Locomotive Works, used at Durnacol. Sold to Rustenburg Platinum Mines, No 5
2064	Dunn's Locomotive Works, used at Durnacol. Sold to Tavistock Colliery, No 3 *Shetlander*
2065	South Witbank Coal Mines No 2 *Pegasus*
2066	Tavistock Colliery No 4 *Highlander*
2067	Tweefontein United Collieries
2068	Tavistock Colliery No 5 *Flying Scotsman*
2069	Rustenburg Platinum Mines No 3
2070	South Witbank Coal Mine No 1 *Zeus*
2071	Rustenburg Platinum Mines No 4

Number series.

SAR Nos	Builder	Date
2060–61	Baldwin	1925
2062–71	Baldwin	1926

Class 15E 4–8–2 Built new for SAR

The class 15E was A. G. Watson's development of the previous 15CA and 15CB classes. Based on the results obtained from using ultra-wide fireboxes on the final batch of 16DA Pacifics, the 15Es also had Wootten type fireboxes. At the time, poppet valves were in their heyday, and these were also incorporated into the design. Powerful and economical when properly handled, these locomotives needed to be maintained properly by knowledgeable fitters who knew how to set the poppet valve gear. In the late 1960s, the whole class was stationed at Bethlehem, where it proved more economical than the later 15F class. However, once put into pool service the locomotives became a liability, and transfers to the Western Cape and Western Transvaal met with little success. One sold out of service to Durnacol Colliery could not be made to work at all until the author managed to scrounge a photostat of the only remaining copy of the poppet valve instructions left in Pretoria!

As at 31 March, the following quantities remained in capital stock:

	1973	1974	1975	1976	1977
	27	24	23	21	nil

Thereafter, the class was considered extinct, but No 2878 has now been resuscitated for enthusiasts' excursions, and after a gap of seven years class 15E again exists, with one example.

As far as running stock is concerned, 1 April 1973 saw one in the Western Cape, and 23 in the Orange Free State, the few running being employed mainly on the Bloemfontein suburban trains. The last was withdrawn in August 1973.

Preservation. No 2878 has been preserved in working order; it is frequently used on enthusiasts' and other specials, and has reappeared in the stock lists.

Industrial. Nos 2872 and 2895 were sold to Dunn's Locomotive Works, and what appears to be an amalgam of the two locomotives was used for a while at Durnacol Colliery, Dannhauser, where it was universally unpopular.

International. Eager to obtain what seemed modern and powerful motive power at bargain prices, two neighbouring countries purchased 15Es, slightly before the period covered in this book, although it is worthwhile placing them on record. Rhodesian Railways hired No 2878 during 1970–71, after which it was returned as defective, although running well enough now. Nos 2881/82/83/85/86/98 were hired to RR in July–August 1970. As at 31 March 1971 they were still SAR property, but within the next year were purchased by RR, retaining their classification and being renumbered simply by reducing the number by 2,000, thus No 2881 became 881, and so on. However, they were destined for a short life in their new country, and were withdrawn and scrapped in 1973, the same year that the SAR survivors became extinct.

The other country which purchased 15Es was Moçambique, which bought three in 1972. Once again, they proved over-complicated for a rather primitive country then in the throes of a war against terrorists, and they seem to have done virtually no work. Renumberings and purchase dates were:

SAR No	CFM No	Date
2870	721	September 1972
2891	722	October 1972
2894	723	August 1972

Details are again by courtesy of the Chief Mechanical Engineer at Lourenço Marques, where they were stationed.

Class 15E No 2891 at Annandale in 1968, shortly before the class was taken off main line service and rapidly relegated to local duties, shunting, and scrap.

Class 15F 4-8-2 Built new for SAR

The class 15F was the piston valve development of the preceding 15E, differing only in the use of these valves, actuated by long travel Walschaerts valve gear. In many ways the 15F became the archetype South African steam locomotive, being the most numerous class built, and almost certainly the most popular amongst footplate staff. Just as handy on anything from express passenger to heavy shunting duties, the locomotives are very much 'maids of all work', and pretty hefty maidens at that, perhaps in line with what Afrikaners term a *boeremeisie*– farmer's daughter!

The earlier examples of the class were hand-fired, but the grate area is rather large for the shovel, although the poppet valve 15E and 16E classes with the same size grate were always hand-fired. The majority of 15Fs were stoker-fired while on main line work, but in latter years when many have been relegated to heavy shunting and trip working, the mechanical stokers have been removed. After withdrawal of the 23 class, large 12-wheel tenders from

Class 15F No 2985 was one of the star locomotives at Springs shed where it is seen easing off the ash pits on a Sunday afternoon in 1979.

scrapped 23s have appeared on many 15Fs, adding considerably to their balanced appearance.

All of the 255 locomotives built were still in capital stock as at 1 April 1973, and for the next ten years numbers decreased slowly due to collision damage only, but from 1982 policy withdrawals commenced.

Over their lives, the 15Fs have been distributed over all but the Cape Eastern systems, and during the period covered the Cape Midland was also devoid of their services, although at one time they dominated the Port Elizabeth main line immediately prior to dieselisation. In the Western Cape, the once medium allocation was mainly for heavy shunting, but also included line work along the branch to Malmesbury. The few allocated to the Northern Cape were mainly for heavy shunting.

The Orange Free State allocation was initially all for main line work, chiefly between Bloemfontein and Kroonstad, but when this line was electrified in 1976, they replaced the 23 class as heavy shunters at these two important junctions, and later also took up shunting duties at Bethlehem, where in 1973 they were allocated for working the line to Bloemfontein. However, even today it is possible to see 15Fs on main line work in the Orange Free State, mainly on pick-up freights and on passenger work between Bloemfontein and Ladybrand. During the 1970s Kroonstad's 15Fs worked the line to Klerksdorp together with the branch to Bultfontein and the link from Whites via Welkom. Even today, they work the short branch to Glen Harmony, formerly the province of the 16DA Pacifics.

Natal was never a great user of 15Fs, being largely Garratt country, but Glencoe had an allocation mainly sub-shedded at Newcastle to work heavy coal traffic on the Utrecht branch.

The largest user today is the Southern Transvaal (formerly Western Transvaal). Serving the highly industrialised Witwatersrand, this system has not only the highest proportion of electrified lines in the country, but also operates the most steam locomotives, an apparent paradox due to the large number of industrial sidings to the shunted, plus proximity to the Witbank coalfield. The large variety of locomotives once found has now been sub-

stantially reduced, with 15Fs predominating, to the main sheds of Germiston, Springs, and Millsite, and their sub-sheds. Indeed, Springs shed, which in the 1970s boasted a dozen classes in an allocation of about 40 locomotives, now has around 50–all class 15F. Line work for 15Fs was principally on the Springs—Breyten line, now largely dieselised, and Springs—Nigel—Heidelburg, now electrified but still with steam on local freights. Grootvlei—Redan is class 15F, with steam workings now extended to Balfour. Otherwise, the class may be seen all along the Witwatersrand, on heavy shunting and on much trip working under the wires, together with shunting as far east as Vandyksdrift, in the Witbank coalfield. Until 1976, class 15F locomotives often powered passenger trains between Springs and Nigel, and until 1977 also hauled the nightly long-distance, all-stations, between Springs and Breyten.

On the Eastern (now Northern) Transvaal system, 15Fs were in 1973 the mainstay of the Pretoria–Pietersburg line, being stationed at each end. Later they were allowed to run further north to Tzaneen and Beit Bridge as track was strengthened, being displaced further south by diesels. As these sections, too, were dieselised the locomotives were as usual relegated to shunting and trip working, with the occasional passenger run to Cullinan. Distribution between the systems as at 1 April was:

Year	1973	1974	1975	1976	1977	1978	1979	1980	1981	1982	1983	1984	1985	1986	1987	1988
Cape Western	9	31	42	42	30	18	18	18	13	13	6	6	–	–	–	–
Cape Northern	10	–	2	2	–	–	–	–	–	–	–	–	–	–	–	–
Orange Free State	94	87	64	74	91	92	92	84	81	81	71	73	70	70	67	56
Natal	9	12	12	16	16	19	–	–	–	–	–	–	–	–	–	–
West Transvaal	60	60	63	62	63	81	103	117	125	129	126	117	105	111	108	73
East Transvaal	72	63	69	55	51	40	31	31	31	27	26	17	9	1	13	–
Active SAR	254	253	252	251	251	250	244	250	250	250	229	213	184	182	188	129
Staged SAR	–	–	–	–	–	–	–	–	–	–	19	22	39	46	34	70
Hired NRZ	–	–	–	–	–	–	6	–	–	–	–	–	–	–	–	–
Totals	254	253	252	251	251	250	250	250	250	250	248	235	223	228	222	199

Preservation. No 15F has yet officially been preserved, but with a surplus of locomotives relative to their duties, several sheds have 'prestige' examples kept in immaculate condition for working special trains.

Industrial. No 15F has been sold for industrial service.

International. Six 15Fs were hired to Rhodesia Railways in October 1978. In June 1979 the system became the Zimbabwe-Rhodesia Railways, and the 15Fs were returned to SAR the following month, being replaced by GMAM Garratts.

Number series.

SAR Nos	Builder	Date
2902–2908	Schwartzkopf	1938
2909–2922	Henschel	1938
2923–2966	North British	1939
2967–2996	Beyer Peacock	1944
2997–3056	North British	1944
3057–3156	North British	1948

Classes 16R and 16CR 4-6-2 Built new for SAR

These two classes were to all intents and purposes identical, being rebuilds of Hendrie's classes 16, 16B, and 16C, all originally having Belpaire fireboxes. These were considerable enlargements of his original Pacifics for Natal, and were very large express engines when built in 1914. As built with 5ft 0in (1,524mm) driving wheels, the ratio of wheel diameter to rail gauge was the same as a standard gauge locomotive having 6ft 9in (2,050mm) wheels, and their tractive effort at 75 per cent boiler pressure exceeded that—at 85 per cent—of Churchward's 4-6-2 No 111 *The Great Bear* on the Great Western; it equalled, also at 85 per cent, that of Gresley's later Great Northern Pacifics. They were in fact quite the most powerful express passenger design built in Great Britain at the time.

Of the three original versions, the class 16 locomotives were devoid of combustion chambers, and had narrow cabs. The 16B locomotives were the same, but with wide cabs having higher roofs, while the 16C had these features plus firebox combustion chambers. When rebuilt with Watson standard boilers the class 16 became 16R, and the 16B and 16C became 16CR, although it is difficult to see why all cannot have had a uniform classification. Just to confuse the issue, some 16Bs on rebuilding had their

number plates altered to 16BR, a class which officially never existed!

By the time that this survey commenced, about one-third of the class was out of active service. Those in the Cape Midland had replaced the older class 10BR on the tightly-timed Uitenhage suburban services, until in turn replaced by the larger 15AR class. Those in the Western Transvaal were by then in shunting and local goods service, their last passenger duties being on the Breyten line in 1967-68, and on the Nigel suburbans, also from Springs shed, in 1969. So sure-footed were these engines that they took to shunting as readily and effectively as they originally hauled the Johannesburg to Cape Town expresses for which they were designed. Some of their last duties at Springs shed involved taking over from the class S2 0-8-0s, specially designed for shunting service, and 35 years junior to the 16R— yet performed with equal or greater effectiveness by these pensioned-off express machines!

Some were even sold for industrial use, where the last remain in service today, and in this connection it is worth recording that two 16CRs sold to Dunn's Locomotive Works found themselves seconded to Durban Navigation Collieries in Natal, where they hauled a colliers' passenger train composed of old

The last of the once-numerous class 16CR Pacifics are ending their days on the surprising duty of ore haulage at St Helena Gold Mines, near Welkom in the Orange Free State.

Year	1973	1974	1975	1976	1977	1978	1979	1980	1981	1982
Capital stock	41	33	33	23	11	9	2	2	2	–
Operating:										
Cape Midland	14	14	13	–	–	–	–	–	–	–
West Transvaal	19	10	9	1	1	–	–	–	–	–
Totals	33	24	22	1	1	–	–	–	–	–

SAR suburban coaches painted blue—re-creating the days when they hauled the forerunner of today's Blue Train.

Stock Totals. SAR's capital stock figures differentiated between the two classes, which did not officially disappear until 1982. More realistic were the operating totals which finished with the last survivor, a shunter at Volksrust.

Preservation. The locomotive preserved by SAR is No 805, which has been 'de-rebuilt' using a shortened 15A boiler. It is mounted outside Johannesburg station, where it represents a locomotive which Ben Schoeman, a former Minister of Transport, is alleged to have worked on when a railway fireman. 16CR No 809 is supposed to be reserved for RSSA Cape Town branch, while No 816 is preserved in the Transport Museum at Heidelburg, Transvaal. 16R No 794 has been preserved at Potchefstroom University while 16CR No 840 has been retained for the National Railway Museum. *Industrial.* A number of 16CRs were sold into industrial service, detailed as right:

SAR No	Industrial user
813	To Dunn's, thence Delmas Colliery, Durnacol, No 2. Withdrawn/scrapped
815	To St Helena Gold Mine, No 6
817	To St Helena Gold Mine, No 5
818	To Dunn's, thence Delmas Colliery, Durnacol, No 3. Withdrawn/scrapped
819	To St Helena Gold Mine, No 2
821	To St Helena Gold Mine, No 1
838	To Klipfontein Organic Products, later St Helena Gold Mine, No 3
839	To St Helena Gold Mine, No 4

The locomotives at St Helena Gold mine do not carry running numbers, the numbers shown being nominal and possibly suspect.

Number series.

Class	Old class	Numbers	Builder	Date
16R	16	790–801	North British	1914
16CR	16B	802– 11	North British	1917
16CR	16C	812– 21	North British	1919
16CR	16C	822– 41	North British	1921

Classes 16D and 16DA 4-6-2 Built new for SAR

These two classes are really three . . . The 16D was the original Baldwin Pacific version of the 15CB, the 4–8–2s being known as 'Big Bills' and the 4–6–2s as 'Big Berthas'. Both had bar frames extending right through from front buffer beams to rear dragbox. The 16DAs, like the 15CAs, had main frames terminating behind the rear coupled axles, behind which was a built-up wide section under the firebox, giving more ashpan room. The final batch of 16DAs had very much wider fireboxes with correspondingly larger grate area, but for some reason these were not given a separate classification (such as 16DB) as warranted, but were known as 16DA (wide firebox). Probably the reason was some mechanically ignorant accountant objecting to the creation of a 'new locomotive class', while happily agreeing to an 'improved' version of an existing type, unaware of the fact that a new class designation costs nothing!

The original 16Ds had for many years been

The classic 16DA No 850, with normal firebox, is preserved at Theunissen, Orange Free State.

allocated to Paarden Eiland shed in Cape Town, working mainly to Malmesbury, and these were phased out soon after the period covered by this book. The 16DAs of both series were allocated to Bloemfontein and Kroonstad in the Free State, where their duties ranged from suburban and local passenger trains, main line pick-up freights, and shunting. Capital stock figures were:

Year	1973	1974	1975	1976	1977	1978	1979
Capital stock							
16D	4	1	1	–	–	–	–
16DA	19	11	11	9	8	8	–
Running stock							
16DA	18	–	–	–	–	–	–

Preservation. 16DA No 850 has been preserved at Theunissen, this being the only representative of the standard firebox version. No fewer than three of the six wide-firebox 16DAs have been preserved, of which No 876 was for many years at Milner Park showgrounds, Johannesburg, and is now a candidate for operating. No 879 is the current operating example for excursions, and No 878 has been overhauled as an apprentice exercise at Bloemfontein workshops, and is thus in excellent condition. There is also a spare wide-firebox boiler in Bloemfontein! 16D No 860 and 16DA No 870 have been retained for the National Railway Museum.

Industrial and international. Four of the Baldwin batch were sold into industrial service, of which No 844 went to Hlobane Colliery in Natal, being soon transferred to Umgala Colliery, where it still exists as No 2. Nos 845, 847 and 848 of the same batch were sold to Wankie Colliery Company in Rhodesia, where they became Nos 5 to 7 in reverse order, having run un-numbered for a while. These worked in the mine's handsome green livery until 1982, when one was cut-up and the other two relegated to stationary boilers. One has now been preserved alongside the main North road at Hwange (formerly Wankie).

Number series.

SAR Class	SAR Nos	Builder	Date
16D	860–61	Baldwin	1925
16D	862–66	Baldwin	1926
16DA	843–50	Baldwin	1929
16DA	868–73	Hohenzollern	1928
16DA*	874–79	Henschel	1930

*Wide firebox

Wide firebox class 16DA No 879 as preserved in running order is often used for enthusiasts' excursions.

Class 16E 4–6–2 Built new for SAR

The 16Es were the most remarkable narrow gauge express passenger locomotives ever built, having the largest driving wheels (6ft 0in diameter) ever placed under a locomotive of less than 'standard' 4ft 8½in gauge, although the Japanese had several hundred Pacifics and Hudsons with 5ft 9in wheels. Apart from their wheel diameter, the 16Es were truly large machines having an all-up weight and tractive effort equal to or exceeding most Pacifics outside North America, while nowhere outside North America was a larger grate to be found on a 4–6–2. On top of this, they had poppet valves, driven by outside rotary shafts.

In theory, the class disappeared just before the period covered by this book, their last regular duties

The preserved class 16E locomotive, restored to original condition without smoke deflectors, is rather out of its usual operating context as it turns on the triangle at Springs shed.

being from Bloemfontein shed in the Orange Free State. However, the preserved locomotive used on special trains was restored to running (but not to capital) stock in 1981 and is allocated to Beaconsfield shed in the Cape Northern system.

Preservation. No 857 is preserved outside Bloemfontein station, and No 858 preserved in working order for specials.

Number series. Nos 854–859 built by Henschel in 1935. All withdrawn 1972.

Classes 19, 19R, 19B and 19BR 4–8–2 Built new for SAR

To match the concept of a bar-frame 4–8–2 (classes 15CA and 15CB) for heavy main line duties, a lighter version was developed for secondary services over light track of 60lb/yd, the basic design being developed steadily over the years to become the standard type for secondary and branch lines. There were four main variants plus several sub-varieties, making quite a complex group of essentially similar locomotives.

The original class 19 amounted to only four locomotives, no doubt considered as a pilot project, and after purchasing the smaller 19A version, dealt with separately, a slightly modified 19B variant appeared. Technically, the 19B differed in having a slightly longer leading bogie wheelbase, due to the original's wheels fouling the cylinder covers on sharp curves, while the 19B could be discerned by the cab, which sloped slightly inboard above the

Class 19B No 1402 at New Largo Colliery, near Witbank. Unlike the maroon-liveried tank engines, the 19B remains black, and has merely exchanged its SAR number plate for the unicorn emblem of Union Corporation, owners of the mine.

waist rail. The basic boiler dimensions were repeated in the standard 1A boiler, which had more superheater elements.

One of each class was rebuilt with the 1A boiler, becoming classes 19R and 19BR respectively, Nos 1367 and 1410.

In their latter years, the 19/19R locomotives were mainly at Empangeni for working the North Coast line and branches, while just before withdrawal some appeared on the Bergville branch. The 19B/19BR version were used almost exclusively over the Lootsberg Pass, between Rosmead and Graaff Reinet, until replaced by 19Ds. One or two were

The sole member of class 19BR, No 1410, at Koloniesplaas siding in 1968.

stationed at Sydenham, and these sometimes appeared on the Grahamstown branch.

Capital and operating annual totals, as at 31 March/1 April are listed below, with 19/19R being entirely in Natal, and 19B/BR all in the Cape Midland system:

Year		1973	1974	1975	1976	1977	1978	1979
Capital	19	3	3	3	2	2	2	2*
	19R	1	1	1	1	–	–	–
	19B	12	11	11	10	7	4	–
	19BR	1	1	1	1	1	–	–
Operating	19	3	2	2	1	–	–	–
	19R	1	1	1	–	–	–	–
	19B	12	10	5	4	–	–	–
	19BR	1	1	–	–	–	–	–

* A solitary 19 remained in capital stock until 1982.

Preservation. Class 19 No 1369 is preserved at Breyten, and Class 19B No 1412 at Middelburg, Cape Province. Class 19 No 1366, the pioneer locomotive, has been retained for the National Railway Museum.

Industrial. Several of these locomotives, including both the rebuilt examples, have been sold out of service to industry as follows:

Class	SAR No	Disposal
19R	1367	Platberg Colliery, Natal, as No 2. Now scrapped
19B	1402	New Largo Colliery, Transvaal, unnumbered, later to Enyati Railway
19B	1407	Loraine Gold Mine, Orange Free State
19B	1409	Loraine Gold Mine, Orange Free State
19BR	1410	Free State Geduld Gold Mine, No 8, later Fregold North No 10
19B	1411	Free State Geduld Gold Mine, No 7, later Fregold North No 11
19B	1413	Fluor for Sasol plant, Transvaal

Number series

SAR Class	SAR Nos	Builder	Date
19	1366–69	Schwartzkopf	1928
19B	1401–14	Schwartzkopf	1930

Classes 19A and 19AR 4–8–2 Built for SAR

The 19A class was a lighter version of class 19, with marginally smaller boiler, smaller cylinders and wheels, the whole ensemble being only four tons less than the 19 class, which hardly seems worth the cost of redesign. All were built by SLM Winterthur, the only Swiss-built locomotives for SAR. Of the 36 locomotives built, five were later rebuilt with the standard 1A boiler, becoming class 19AR. Of these rebuilds, Nos 678 and 696 had domeless boilers from early class 19D locomotives, as possibly had No 700, the first to be scrapped, in 1966.

The classes were slow to be written-off the capital stock, although all were out of use by 1976. Most of

Class 19A No 691 on the turning triangle at Bergville in October 1972.

the class were in the Eastern Cape, at East London and Queenstown sheds, often sub-shedded to Burgersdorp for branch lines in the area. The Natal locomotives were at Mason's Mill, sub-shedded to Estcourt for the Bergville branch, and at Glencoe sub-shedded to Newcastle for the Utrecht branch, plus a couple of late arrivals in the Western Transvaal.

Capital stock was:

Year	1973	1974	1975	1976	1977	1978	1979	1980	1981	1982	1983	1984
19A	30	28	28	25	19	11	5	3	3	3	3	–
19AR	4	3	3	1	1	–	–	–	–	–	–	–

The dark morning mist rolls away in the background, leaving domeless class 19AR spotlighted at Witbank Consolidated Colliery in the winter of 1983.

Running stock was divided as below:

Year		1973	1974	1975	1976	1977
Cape Eastern	19A	18	13	–	–	–
	19AR	2	1	–	–	–
Natal	19A	10	8	3	2	–
	19AR	1	1	–	–	–
West Transvaal	19A	2	–	–	–	–
	19AR	1	–	–	–	–

Preservation. Class 19A No 692 is preserved at Sterkstroom.

Industrial. The following have been sold into industrial use:

Class	SAR No	Disposal
19AR	678	Tweefontein United Collieries, later Witbank Consolidated Collieries
19A	679	Apex Mines, Greenside, later to Fluor for Sasol plant, later to Dunn's. True identity of this locomotive thought to be No 697
19A	683	Tweefontein United Collieries, now withdrawn
19A	684	Gledhow Sugar Mill, *Umvoti.* Sold to Umgala Colliery
19A	689	Platberg Colliery, scrapped
19A	691	Gledhow Sugar Mill, No 2 *Blythedale*
19A	707	Platberg Colliery, No 1. Now scrapped
19A	710	Butakon Ltd. Thence Southern Cross Steel Co, Middelburg (Transvaal), now at Umgala Colliery, Utrecht No 3

Number series.

Nos 675–710 SLM Winterthur, 1929, class 19A.

Nos 678, 693, 696, 700 & 706 rebuilt to class 19AR.

Class 19C 4–8–2 Built new for SAR

The original specification for these locomotives was for a further 50 of class 19B, but during the tendering period North British suggested the use of RC poppet valves, this proposal being accepted by SAR. The new classification, 19C, was only decided upon about the time of delivery. Apart from the valve gear, the locomotives from the outset incorporated the standard 1A boiler, with larger superheater, while the cab was altered to the sloping front design standard on later SAR classes. With their poppet valves, they proved very free-running engines, although requiring special maintenance techniques.

As a result, the whole class spent their last years in the Western Cape, based at Paarden Eiland shed, Cape Town, and used mainly along the lengthy branch line to Bitterfontein, and to a lesser extent to Caledon and Protem.

Several detail variations were evident in later years. Some had domeless boilers from early 19D engines, these boilers probably appearing on different engines due to exchanges during overhaul,

A class 19C locomotive pauses at a wayside station on the Bitterfontein line about 1975, shortly before the line went over to diesel operation.

but No 2480 was one fitted. Most had small boxes for ash-catching, just below the smokebox front, and No 2456 for a short period had the chimney extended backwards of the boiler, bifurcated, to exhaust through two outlets just ahead of the cab! Several locomotives had large tenders, mounted on two six-wheel bogies, and with cylindrical water tanks.

Capital, active, and staged figures, all for Western Cape, were as shown below.

Preservation. No 2439 is effectively 'preserved', but remains on the capital list and was used initially for excursions in the Western Cape. Later transferred to Krugersdorp and currently on the Eastern Cape.

Industrial. Poppet valves, and the long distance from industry prevented any being sold for this purpose.

Number series.

Nos 2435–2484. Built North British, 1935.

Year	1973	1974	1975	1976	1977	1978	1979	1980	1981	1982	1983	1984
Capital	50	50	50	50	49	49	49	22	1	1	1	1
Active	50	50	50	48	1	1	1	1	1	1	1	1
Staged	–	–	–	–	47	–	–	–	–	–	–	–

Only a few class 19C locomotives ran with domeless boilers, as this withdrawn example on Touwsrivier dump.

Wardale's modified class 19D No 2644 at Belmont in 1979 on an early test trip. Smoke deflectors have been added, and running plate lowered adjacent to the firebox to clear secondary air ducts. A small tender is still attached.

Class 19D 4–8–2 Built for SAR

The 19D was the final development of the 19th series locomotives, and was developed by the new chief mechanical engineer, Mr W. A. J. Day, who was not a believer in poppet valves. This class thus reverted to the piston valves and Walschaerts valve gear of the earlier 19 to 19B classes. However, the cylinders were redesigned with straighter steam ports, and the valve gear similarly revamped with longer steam lap and greater travel – indeed, the greatest values of these dimensions used on a new SAR locomotive design.

The design earned great popularity, and became the most numerous SAR class for secondary services; the total built, at 235, was only 20 fewer than the 15F, the country's most numerous steam class. With such large numbers, the class was widespread throughout SAR with the exception of the Western Cape, which used class 19C for such duties. The only allocations to this system were purely nominal, to cover locomotives staged out of service. Duties

Approaching the summit of Lootsberg Pass two class 19D locomotives on a northbound freight negotiate one of four similar curves on the 1 in 40 climb.

covered by the class were widespread, varying from main line international passenger trains between Warrenton and Mafeking, through the expected range of secondary and branch line duties to, in later years, such menial tasks as shed and works shunters. A list of lines worked by class 19D locomotives would be tedious.

Remarkably few variations occurred, for such a large class. About 40 early examples had domeless boilers, otherwise identical to the standard 1A fitted to the rest of the class, and as these boilers were fully interchangeable they gradually became used also on later 19D, and on some 19C and 19AR. The final batch of fifty 19D had twelve-wheel 'torpedo' tenders, with cylindrical tanks, some of which found their way to the 19C class.

Finally, No 2644 was modified in 1979 by D. Wardale, and details of this modification and the results therefrom are found in Chapter 7.

Heavy overhauls are still being carried out on class 19D at SAR's Uitenhage workshops, and examples of the class will probably see out the end of steam. Capital and distribution figures over the years are:

Year	1973	1974	1975	1976	1977	1978	1979	1980	1981	1982	1983	1984	1985	1986	1987	1988
Capital	235	235	235	235	234	234	234	232	230	230	230	156	143	143	158	105
Operating stock																
Cape North	59	57	65	60	59	59	59	72	67	41	43	23	21	19	18	16
Cape Midland	29	42	38	38	38	38	45	35	38	30	32	36	34	28	29	23
Cape Eastern	26	26	26	28	31	31	28	29	29	23	7	–	–	–	1	1
Orange Free State	48	48	52	55	50	50	45	39	40	28	20	22	21	21	16	10
Natal	7	11	8	8	8	8	2	2	3	–	–	–	–	–	–	–
West Transvaal	2	2	8	16	22	22	22	24	24	18	18	–	3	3	3	3
East Transvaal	64	49	37	29	23	22	21	23	24	26	19	16	5	–	11	5
Active	235	235	234	234	231	230	228	225	225	166	139	97	84	71	78	58
Staged	–	–	–	–	3	4	4	4	4	63	90	56	59	72	80	47
Hired (Zimbabwe)	–	–	–	–	–	–	–	1	–	–	–	–	–	–	–	–
Hired (Moçambique)	–	–	–	–	–	–	6	–	–	–	–	–	–	–	–	–

Preservation. Five 19D have been preserved, No 2510 at Barkly East, No 2541 at Potgietersrust, No 2526 at Railcar, Welkom, No 2646 reserved for RSSA Cape Town, and No 2725 at Coligny. In addition, No 2540 and No 3322 have been allocated to the National Railway Museum, as may be No 2749 blue painted for shunting. *Blue Train* stock at Pretoria, and rebuilt engine No 2644 used for special workings.

Industrial, regional. Several 19D have been sold to industry, and this number is likely to increase. To date, the following are relevant:

No 2513 Dunn's, later Saiccor No 1
No 2633 Saiccor No 2
No 2654 Loraine Gold Mine
No 2657 Bamangwato Concessions, Botswana, No V
No 2697 Saiccor
No 2767 Saiccor
No 3350 Bamangwato Concessions, Botswana.

International. The 19D is undoubtedly the widest known steam class in southern Africa. At one time the locomotives worked through from Mafeking in South Africa, through Botswana (then Bechuanaland) to Bulawayo, while SAR members of the class also were hired, as seen from the table above, to Beit Bridge in Zimbabwe, and to Maputo in Moçambique, in each case for shunting.

This was far from being the end of things international. Rhodesia Railways purchased 21 of the class from Henschel, one of which was originally a condensing locomotive. Tenders were similar to the SAR 'torpedo' type, but had plate instead of buckeye bogies. Six were built for the Benguela railway in Angola, these being perhaps the best-looking, with handsome cabs and chimneys. Finally, six were built for industrial service—two for the Nkana copper mines in Northern Rhodesia (now Zambia), and four without superheaters for Wankie Colliery in Rhodesia. Including these foreign versions, there were 262 built to the 19D design, making them more numerous than SAR's 15F class.

Number series.

SAR Nos	Builder	Date
2506–2525	Krupp	1937
2526–2545	Borsig	1937
2626–2640	Skoda	1938
2641–2652	Krupp	1938
2653–2680	Krupp	1939
2681–2720	Borsig	1938–39
2721–2770	R. Stephenson	1945
3321–3370	North British	1948

Class 23 4–8–2 Built for SAR

Year	1973	1974	1975	1976	1977	1978	1979	1980	1981	1982	1983	1984	1985	1986
Capital	123	122	121	119	112	112	106	106	106	106	106	4	3	1
Operating:														
Cape Northern	25	–	–	–	–	–	–	–	–	–	–	–	–	–
Free State	97	121	120	110	66	65	65	65	65	1	1	1	1	1
Staged	–	–	–	–	41	41	41	41	41	105	105	2	2	–

Class 23 was the largest and latest 4–8–2 design for SAR, although numbers of classes 15F and 19D were built after the last 23 had been completed. As originally designed, the class 23 locomotives were to have 5ft 6in coupled wheels, as a halfway stage between the 5ft 0in of the 15F and the 6ft 0in wheels of the 16E classes. This seems to have been the intention up to quite a late stage, as the cylinders were cast to suit such a wheel diameter. However, it was decided to reduce the wheel diameter in order to shorten the coupled wheelbase to ease passage on curves.

Due mainly to fatigue cracks in the bar frames, the class 23s were withdrawn from main line service considerably earlier than the similar 15F class. In 1973 they were working traffic on the Kimberley–De Aar line, from which they were soon replaced by class 25 and 25NC 4–8–4s. Most were in the Orange Free State, working the bulk of traffic between Bloemfontein and Kroonstad until replaced by 15Fs. Thereafter, the class was used mainly on heavy shunting at those two depots, plus some local goods work, until again replaced by 15Fs made redundant by electrification. Most were staged under the 'strategic reserve' programme, many at Beaufort West where they had a nominal allocation to the Cape Western system. Others were dumped at their last working sheds, and many have ceded their large twelve-wheel tenders to increase the range of 15Fs still at work.

Capital and operating details are shown above.

Preservation. No 3300 is kept in working order as a prestige engine at Kroonstad shed, for working specials. No 2556 is preserved at Touwsrivier and No 3286 at Bloemfontein shed.

Number series.

SAR Nos	Builder	Date
2552–2558	Schwartzkopf	1938
2559–2571	Henschel	1938
3201–3285	Henschel	1938
3286–3316	Schwartzkopf	1938–39

With only 3in (76mm) more driving wheel diameter, the class 23 managed to look more of an express engine than the sturdy class 15F.

Class 24 2–8–4 Built for SAR

Class 24 No 3651, employed on the branch to Ladysmith, sits under the coaling stage at Touwsrivier in 1979.

Reversing SAR's most popular wheel arrangement, the Class 24 was designed with an 11½-ton axle load to permit running on track of 45lb/yd. Despite this restriction, the locomotives feature cast-steel bed frames and the same boiler as class 19D, but with a shorter barrel. Built to replace the old 7th and 8th classes of 4–8–0, most were initially assigned to South West Africa where they hauled main line traffic, but subsequently they have been used mainly on lightly-laid branches. Being relatively powerful, they are also useful suburban engines, and were used on the Springs–Nigel service prior to electrification.

Distribution has been wide throughout SAR, with the notable exception of Natal, and branches which saw them in multiple were George to Knysna, Breyten to Lothair, Nylstroom to Vaalwater and Port Elizabeth to Alexandra. The class is still receiving heavy overhauls at Bloemfontein, and should last to the end of steam.

Preserved. No 3608 is preserved in Calvinia, and No 3638 in the Kruger National Park at Skukuza. No 3675 was the 2000th locomotive built by North British for SAR, and is named *Bartholomew Diaz*. The engine is currently retained in working order for special trains at Krugersdorp, and Nos 3611–12 have been transferred to Windhoek for similar workings, the first working steam in the territory for nearly thirty years.

Number series.
Nos 3601–3700, built North British 1949–50.

Year	1973	1974	1975	1976	1977	1978	1979	1980	1981	1982	1983	1984	1985	1986	1987	1988
Cape Western	21	21	21	29	34	34	34	34	32	3	1	1	1	1	–	–
Cape Northern	12	13	13	13	13	13	13	13	14	6	4	5	5	1	1	–
Cape Midland	25	28	28	30	30	30	30	30	31	31	23	22	24	26	24	19
Cape Eastern	4	4	4	4	4	4	4	4	4	4	3	–	–	–	–	–
Orange Free State	9	–	–	–	–	–	–	–	–	–	–	–	–	–	–	–
West Transvaal	15	19	16	6	–	–	–	–	–	–	–	–	–	1	13	1
East Transvaal	14	15	18	18	18	18	17	17	17	21	21	22	20	17	1	–
Total	100	100	100	100	99	99	98	98	98	65	52	50	50	46	39	20
Staged	–	–	–	–	19*	21*	21*	21*	21*	22	43	8	7	13	25	18
Capital	100	100	100	100	100	100	99	98	98	98	97	58	58	58	64	38

* figures included in the system totals

Classes 25, 25NC, and 26 4–8–4 Built for SAR

These 4–8–4s were the final main line tender engines built for SAR, and in mechanical features are the most modern running anywhere in the World today. As originally conceived, the design was no more than an extended 15F, with larger boiler and four-wheel trailing truck, but in the gestation period leading up to manufacture, cast-steel bed frames were decided upon together with roller bearings on all axles and crankpins, features which raised the locomotives' mechanical performance well above anything else on SAR. Unfortunately, some of the 15F thinking remained, including the steam lap and valve travel, smaller valves than used on the 19D class. Also, despite the design's larger overall size, it had no more adhesion weight than class 15F, and would have been better either with greater axle loading or as a 2–10–4. Within these limitations, the locomotives are mechanically excellent, although not so efficient as the later European steam designs.

The majority of 90 were built as condensing engines, where exhaust steam was returned to the tender and cooled back to water, which proved very useful over the dry Karoo areas through which they originally worked. However, this equipment proved expensive to maintain. Fifty were built without condensing equipment, and these became class 25NC. After twenty years' service, the spread of electrification and diesel-isation over routes used by condensing class 25 led to a decision to convert the class to 25NC, the first two being done at running sheds. Beaconsfield converted No 3452, the tender having a similar profile to the later standard, but with a curious 'poop deck' around the tank filler. No 3468, converted at De Aar, had a tender of similar

The last southbound Drakensberg Express is seen accelerating south of Kimberley behind condenser 4–8–4 No 3462 in May 1978, The massive motive power and immaculate trackwork put many a broader gauge railway to shame.

A summer afternoon in 1981 finds the Trans Karoo Express speeding into the dusk behind rebuilt condenser 4–8–4 No 3537.

Class 26 No 3450, officially named L. D. Porta but invariably known as 'The Red Devil' due to its livery, is seen at Bethlehem shed in 1982.

Year	1973	1974	1975	1976	1977	1978	1979	1980	1981	1982	1983	1984	1985	1986	1987	1988
Class 25 condensing																
Cape Western	64	8	–	–	–	–	–	–	–	–	–	–	–	–	–	–
Cape Northern	26	82	81	64	39	27	14	2	2	1	1	1	1	1	1	1
Class 25NC																
Cape Western	–	–	–	–	–	–	–	–	–	–	–	1	1	1	–	–
Cape Northern	50	50	37	54	79	91	100	112	112	112	110	109	107	107	105	105
Orange Free State	–	–	22	22	22	22	26	25	25	25	26	24	24	24	23	23
Staged	–	–	–	–	–	–	–	–	–	–	1	–	1	1	–	–
Class 26																
Cape Northern	–	–	–	–	–	–	–	–	–	1	1	1	1	1	1	1

profile to the original condensing version, but with the radiator vents filled-in. The final conversion featured a long, low, D-shape tank, it being impracticable to shorten the tender due to the mainframe being a single 'waterbottom' casting. Series conversion to non-condensing commenced in 1974 and was complete in 1980, other than three locomotives which were not converted.

The final development of the class was in 1981 when 25NC No 3450 was outshopped from Salt River works completely rebuilt and reclassified 26, although usually known as the 'Red Devil' due to the livery applied. The extensive modifications substantially increased both the power output and efficiency, and further details will be found in the chapter concerning steam development.

During the period under review, the condensers were mainly stationed at Beaufort West, from which they almost monopolised the line to De Aar. Others were at Beaconsfield, running from Kimberley to De Aar or Bloemfontein. When the line south from De Aar was dieselised during 1973–74, the condensing locomotives were moved north to both De Aar and Kimberley, enabling 22 non-condensing to transfer to Bethlehem in the Free State. By this stage, 4–8–4s handled most traffic in the three stages from Bethlehem to De Aar, a situation which largely continues today. However, the gradual infiltration of diesels released

further 4–8–4s, and from 1982 they started working from Warrenton to Vryburg, and in 1984 extended these workings to Mafikeng (formerly Mafeking) taking over from 19D and GMAM classes.

The 25NCs continue to receive heavy overhauls at Bloemfontein, and are expected to run into the 1990s. Distribution over the years is shown above.

Preservation. Condenser No 3451 has been retained for static exhibition, and No 3511 as an operating locomotive. 25NCs No 3414 and 3481 are destined for the National Railway Museum together with class 26 No 3450 *The Red Devil*.

Number series.

Class	SAR Nos	Builder	Date
25NC	3401–3411	North British	1954
25NC	3412–3450	Henschel	1953
25	3451	Henschel	1953
25	3452–3540	North British	1953–54

All the condensing tenders were built by Henschel.

Glinting in the later afternoon sun, a class 25NC locomotive rounds the well-known curve at Meynell, scene of so many photographic disappointments as sunset or evening cloud so often obscure the sun just before the train appears in the viewfinder.

Class GCA 2-6-2 + 2-6-2 Garratt

These were the smallest 3ft 6in gauge Garratts used during the currency of this book, and were developed from the original GC class built by Beyer Peacock with plate frames. The GCAs were built by Krupp, and had bar frames, while the fireboxes were round-topped as opposed to the GCs Belpaires. Round-front tanks and built-up bunkers gave these little Garratts quite a distinctive appearance, and they were relatively speedy despite their minute driving wheels.

By 1973, the 39 original members of the class had dwindled to seven, all stationed at Mason's Mill, Pietermaritzburg, for use on the lightly-laid Underberg branch, where they were often used in pairs. By April 1973 their numbers had dropped to five, all of which lasted until October 1975, when the class became extinct. One of their last duties was the operation of re-railing trains, laying the heavier rails which enabled diesels to replace them.

SAR's class GCA Garratts were the smallest 3ft 6in gauge articulated locomotives to survive into the 1970s.

Preservation. No 2196 is preserved at White River, and No 2621 at Nelspruit, both in the Eastern Transvaal, where once they worked. No 2199 is reserved for the National Railway Museum.
Industrial. A few were sold into industrial use prior to the currency of this book, but none survived.

Number series.

SAR Nos	Builder	Date
2190–2202	Krupp	1927
2600–2625	Krupp	1928

Class GE 2–8–2 + 2–8–2 Garratt

These were the first eight-coupled Garratts built for SAR, and at the time of building were, on a tractive effort basis, the most powerful locomotives in the Southern Hemisphere. Plate frames formed the basis for these heavy sloggers, whose piston valve cylinders were fed with super-heated steam from the Belpaire boiler. The three series built were visibly distinguishable, the first series having the old all-square 'cistern' type front tank, while over the years the original low bunkers had been built-up in various manners until each, perhaps, differed. The second series had rounded top corners to the front tanks, and an inset coal bunker for better visibility. The third series, of two locomotives only, differed technically in having larger diameter cylinders, which were indistinguishable, but were visually different in having cabs slightly wider below the waistrails, the upper panels being equally slightly tapered inboard.

The final duties for the GE class were on the Nkwalini branch in Natal, where they were replaced by GEA and GO classes. Ten out of the

The only survivor of class GE is the prototype, No 2260, preserved beside Empangeni station.

original 18 locomotives were still in active stock in March 1975, but all had gone a month later.

Preservation. The first of class, No 2260, is preserved at Empangeni station.

Industrial. Rather surprisingly, none of these useful, low-speed sloggers, found its way into industrial service.

Number series.

Batch	SAR Nos	Builder	Date
I	2260–65	Beyer Peacock	1924–25
II	2266–75	Beyer Peacock	1926
III	2276–77	Beyer Peacock	1930

International. The GE class design was used for the Sierra Leone Development Corporation railway in West Africa.

Class GEA No 4004 simmers outside Empangeni shed.

Class GEA 4–8–2 + 2–8–4 Garratt

These were the largest hand-fired Garratts on SAR in recent years and their classification indicates a route of development from the earlier GE class, having similar wheel diameter and similar overall boiler dimensions. However, apart from such nominal considerations, the design was thoroughly revised to include an expanded wheel arrangement, bar instead of plate frames, round-top instead of Belpaire fireboxes, and a host of other improvements and variations. It is possible that the otherwise blank class, GN, may have been considered for this class, but no confirmation has been forthcoming. Visible variations within the class include at least three bunker variations, while No 4009 was at one time the experimental spark-arresting locomotive named *Renoster*.

At the beginning of this book's coverage, all but two of the original 50 locomotives were still at work, those in the Cape Western being stationed at Paarden Eiland shed for working over Sir Lowry's Pass to Caledon, from whence they were replaced by diesels. The Cape Midland ones were at Voorbaai, and worked to Riversdale and Oudtshoorn before replacement by GMAM Garratts, while the Natal locomotives were at Stanger and Empangeni, working the North Coast main line, and the Eshowe and Nkwalini branches until replaced variously by newer Garratts, diesels, and electrification, all in rather a hurried jumble.

The final rundown by areas was:

As at 1 April	1973	1974	1975	1976	1977
Cape Western	18	17	23	16	nil
Cape Midland	15	15	9	nil	nil
Natal	15	16	14	nil	nil
Total	48	48	46	16	nil

The last 16 locomotives were withdrawn during August 1976, but the final 'big show' for the class was during the 1975 Cape fruit season, when the standard motive power over Sir Lowry's Pass was a GEA piloted by a 14CRB 4–8–2.

Preservation. No 4022 is reserved for the National Railway Museum.

Industrial. The following have been sold into industrial service:

SAR No	Disposal
4003	Dunn's Locomotive Works. Hired in Witbank area
4020	Dunn's Locomotive Works. Used at Enyati Colliery, later to Vryheid Coronation Colliery.
4023	Vryheid Coronation Colliery No 6
4024	Dunn's Locomotive Works. Hired in Witbank area, scrapped.
4027	Dunn's Locomotive Works. Used at Enyati Colliery, scrapped.
4031	Vryheid Coronation Colliery No 5.

Number series.
No 4001–50, Beyer Peacock, 1946.

Class GF 4–6–2 + 2–6–4 Garratt Built for SAR

From its introduction until the building of the GMA/ M classes, the GF was the most numerous Garratt class in the world. Sixty-five were built, all in Germany, and their 4ft 6in driving wheels and 14-ton axle load made them very useful all-purpose machines for secondary and branch lines. During the course of their long lives they have seen service over much of SAR's entire system.

Apart from four sold to Moçambique and two scrapped due to collisions, all were in stock in 1972, although not all in operation. The locomotives in the Eastern Transvaal were stationed at Nelspruit, from where they worked the branches to Graskop and Plaston, while the bulk were in Natal. Some of the Natal locomotives were at Empangeni, working mainly sugar cane traffic to Mtubatuba, while the biggest allocation was at Mason's Mill shed for the various branches radiating from Pietermaritzburg. All were withdrawn from these final sheds, and no major reallocations occurred. Figures in stock and in service are tabulated below.

Preservation. No 2380 is preserved at Frankfort, Orange Free State, and No 2401 has been retained for the National Railway Museum. This latter locomotive was painted dark blue while at Nelspruit, retaining this livery after transfer to Mason's Mill. No 2416 has also been retained for the National Railway Museum.
Industrial. A surprising number of GFs were sold into mining service where a fairly light and large-

Class GF No 2395 has a Sunday rest at the little Zululand locomotive outpost of Mtubatuba.

wheel type seemed hardly the most suitable. Most of those sold were to the Enyati Railway, where No 2371 was once resplendent in maroon livery, lined out in yellow. In later days, the surviving Enyati engines were fitted with diesel-driven air-brake equipment sited in a 'cage' behind the bunker. On the Enyati line, double-heading was common from Boomlager to the *nek* at the summit, with triple-heading occurring on several occasions. On reverse journeys, with loaded trains, banking was employed from the *nek* to the first summit, and various weird combinations occurred, of which the most outlandish seen by the author was a train headed by a single GF followed by a rake of air-braked wagons, two more GFs, and finally several vacuum-braked wagons! At the water stop over the summit, this cavalcade was broken into an air-braked train, light engine, and vacuum-braked train, for final descent to Boomlager. Due to the removal of both number and maker's plates from locomotives when sold, some of the identities are vague, but as far as is known locomotives worked as follows:
Enyati Railway. Nos 2371, 2377, 2378, 2386, 2387, 2399, 2404, 2408, 2415, 2417, 2425, 2429.
Transvaal Navigation Collieries. No 2433.
Tweefontein United Collieries. An unidentified locomotive, believed later transferred to Enyati.

Number series.

Year	1973	1974	1975	1976	1977	1978	1979	1980
Capital	54	45	43	41	28	22	17	–
Operating								
Natal	28	29	11	–	–	–	–	–
East Transvaal	19	–	–	–	–	–	–	–
Total	47	29	11	–	–	–	–	–

SAR Nos	Builder	Date
2370–2406	Hanomag	1927–28
2407–24	Henschel	1928
2425–34	Maffei	1928

Class GM 4-8-2 + 2-8-4 Garratt

Class GM Garratt No 2303 soon after arrival at Durnacol, Dannhauser. It is fitted with a tender from an old class 1 locomotive, in lieu of a 'torpedo' tank.

The GM class was the large, light axle-load Garratt developed before World War II, based largely on the enormous GL class. Subsequently the GM design was modernised to form the basis for the GMA/M and GO classes. For most of their lives the locomotives worked between Johannesburg or Krugersdorp and Mafeking but in 1973, having been replaced by diesels, they had been transferred to Pretoria and Pietersburg, sheds unused to Garratts and where their presence as hand-me-downs made them doubly unpopular. Thus at 1 April 1973 eleven were officially in stock although they hardly turned a wheel, and by 1 August all were officially withdrawn.

This is where the story takes a Quixotic turn, such as to cast doubt on those meticulous historians who take great pains to verify 'official figures', for in mid-1973, just as the last GM had been officially withdrawn, several accidents created a shortage of GMA/M Garratts in the Eastern Transvaal. To keep traffic moving, GMs Nos 2301/03/04 were given a quick light overhaul at Capital Park, and despatched to Breyten to fill the motive power vacuum. They worked at Breyten for about a year, initially taking part in the regular main line workings down to Piet Retief, but later descending to the short pickups to Ermelo, and the Spitzkop colliery shunt. Never in this time did they appear on the official motive power returns, and traffic was presumably recorded as being moved by locomotives which on

paper did not exist! When the GMA/M position returned to normal, the three GMs were quietly retired and offered for sale by tender, being purchased by Dunn's Locomotive Works, which hired them out to various mines as detailed below:

Preservation. No 2292 was retained for preservation in the official SAR scheme, but was subsequently taken off the list. Surviving at Millsite shed, it may be incorporated into the RSSA collection.

Industrial. As detailed above, three GMs were sold into industry, and used for several years.

No 2301 Sold to Dunn's, went to Douglas Colliery 11/75 and used with old tender ex Mallet MC1 No 1643. Ceased work early 1977, but still on site.

No 2303 Sold to Dunn's and hired to Durnacol, where it ran until about 1978, coupled to an old class 1 tender.

No 2304 Sold to Dunn's, and hired firstly to Transvaal Navigation Collieries. Transferred to Tweefontein United Colliery in July 1977, but disused soon after. Still in existence on Dunn's dump at Witbank.

Number series.
Nos 2291–2306. Beyer Peacock, 1938

Class GMA and GMAM 4–8–2 + 2–8–4 Garratt

The GMA and GMAM were virtually identical classes, differing only in the amount of coal and water carried, and the physical arrangements involving the re-arrangement of baffles in externally identical front tank and bunker. On the GMA, 1,650 gallons of water and 11·6 tons of coal sufficed for a maximum axle load of 15·35 tons, enabling them to run on track of 60lb/yd. The GMAM (the final M denoting 'Main line', carried 2,100 gallons of water and 14 tons of coal, increasing the axle load marginally to 15·7 tons and the total locomotive weight by 4·35 tons, thereby by a very pedantic margin making them too heavy for 60lb/yd rail. A considerably greater coal, water, and adhesion capacity would have been easy to achieve and far more useful.

Although based on the pre-war GM class, with which the basic dimensions tallied, the GMAM was in fact a far more modern design, having cast-steel engine beds with integral cylinders, roller bearings on all axles, but lacking this feature on the crankpins. The 120 members of the class constituted the most numerous Garratt class in the World, and up to 1962 the locomotives were divided into 20 GMA

The last major outpost for regular GMAM workings is Randfontein Estates Gold Mines, where No R12 Barbara is seen newly outshopped in maroon and gold.

and 100 GMAM. Conversion to GMA steadily proceeded until by 1969 there were 69 GMA and 49 GMAM, two having by then been scrapped due to collisions. During the period covered by this book, reconversion to GMAM took place and the situation as at 1 April each year in this period was as below. These were the capital stock figures, and in the later years many were out of use.

Being a powerful, yet light axle load design, the GMA/M locomotives have found widespread use over the system, often being the final steam power used immediately before dieselisation or electrification. Unfortunately, they became something of hand-me-down locomotives, being in later years in run-down condition and unpopular with crews, although capable of excellent performance when well maintained. During their days of being largely surplus to requirements some were hired to Zimbabwe and Moçambique.

Within South Africa, GMA/Ms were used over

Year	1973	1974	1975	1976	1977	1978	1979	1980	1981	1982	1983	1984
GMA	70	70	25	25	25	24	24	24	24	24	23	5
GMAM	48	48	93	90	87	87	87	87	87	84	78	25

many routes, with a majority in Natal at the beginning of the period covered, later transfers giving the maximum number to the Cape Midland system. In Natal, the bulk of the locomotives were at first in Pietermaritzburg (Mason's Mill) from where they worked most trains on the two heavily-graded branches to Greytown and Franklin. Some were on the North coast line, working between Stanger and Empangeni, and on both these sections double-heading with each other and with other Garratt classes was common. After 1976–77 most were transferred away, other than a couple at Mason's Mill which performed heavy shunting and transfer duties, which meant that they were fortunately on hand to work the centenary train from Durban to Pietermaritzburg in 1980.

The Cape Western locomotives were stationed at Worcester and worked the line to Riversdale until dieselisation. Late in the day the Cape Northern system acquired an allocation for working the

Vryburg–Mafeking line, on which they were used from 1981 until early 1984, this being their last main line service. Here they largely replaced the class 19D which formerly dominated the line, although double-heading with 19Ds and other GMAMs was not uncommon. Laying of heavy rail enabled them to be replaced by class 25NC 4–8–4s in 1984.

The Cape Midland system became home for the bulk of the class for a fairly short period, and at first the locomotives were stationed at Voorbaai to replace the GEA class on trains from Mossel Bay to Riversdale and to Oudtshoorn. Later their allocation was extended to Sydenham, Rosmead, Klipplaat, and Graaff Reinet sheds so that GMA/Ms were to be found working most trains over the route from Port Elizabeth to Rosmead via Klipplaat. Indeed, during this period, of the 1,085km run from Cape Town to Port Elizabeth, 910km was steam-powered, of which 662km was with GMA/M Garratts. The most spectacular steam-powered mountain passes, the Montagu and the Lootsberg, were then worked by this class.

The other system which had a GMA/M allocation was the Eastern Transvaal, where Waterval Boven and Breyten sheds operated the line down to Vryheid in Natal. Here the locomotives were re-

Year	1973	1974	1975	1976	1977	1978	1979	1980	1981	1982	1983	1984	1985	1986	1987	1988
Cape Western	13	13	17	18	18	18	20	8	3	–	–	–	–	–	–	–
Cape Northern	–	–	–	–	–	–	–	–	2	10	14	–	–	–	–	
Cape Midland	–	–	27	49	52	55	59	40	27	–	–	–	2	2	2	2
Natal	80	78	36	12	6	2	2	3	4	2	2	–	–	–	–	–
East Transvaal	25	25	35	35	36	36	37	61	13	10	10	7	8	4	1	1
Total SAR	118	116	115	114	112	111	111	88	97	25	26	9	10	6	3	3
Staged SAR	–	–	–	–	–	–	1	1	–	76	67	34	32	34	78	9
Hired Zimbabwe	–	–	–	–	–	–	–	22	6	–	–	–	–	–	–	–
Hired Moçambique	–	–	–	–	–	–	–	–	8	7	6	–	–	–	–	–
Total stock	118	116	115	114	112	111	111	111	111	108	99	43	42	40	81	12

placed by diesels, but Waterval Boven, even at the time of writing, uses Garratts for shunting and the occasional trip down the line to Carolina, where once they double-headed on coal trains. These are the last GMA/M workings on the South African Transport Services. During 1975 some of Waterval Boven's Garratts were sub-shedded at Derwent (normally sub to Witbank) for use on the Roossenekal branch, later electrified. Capital Park shed in Pretoria was also the nominal home for Garratts hired to Zimbabwe and Moçambique during 1980–83. These returned to SA for major repairs, and Capital Park sometimes used them on its own turns, particularly heavy ballast workings, and even at times the Cullinan passenger trains.

During the 1980s, as the class was progressively withdrawn from service, many of the locomotives were accumulated on the dump at De Aar, known as the 'strategic reserve', but in 1984 these started to be written-off for sale or scrapping. Nominal distribution of the class at 1 April was as shown above.

Preservation. No 4112 has been donated to the 4160 Ltd group in England, and was shipped from South Africa in 1984. Nos 4070 and 4072 at Voorbaai, and No 4122 at Witbank, the only operating examples, are retained just for special trains.

Industrial. Several GMA/M have been sold into industrial service including 4090 and 4129 which have been sold to the Hothan Valley Railway in Western Australia, where they will haul tourists in ex-SAR passenger coaches. They will have the lightest nominal tractive effort (at 85%) of any Australian steam locomotive, irrespective of rail gauge!

SAR No	Disposal
4059	Randfontein Estates GM No R16 *Sarah*
4060	Randfontein Estates GM No R15 (first) *May.* Scrapped
4073	Randfontein Estates GM No R17 *Coria*
4079	Randfontein Estates GM No R15 (second) *May*
4084	Randfontein Estates GM No R10 scrapped
4107	Randfontein Estates GM No R14 (first) *Cherrie*
4108	Tweefontein Colliery
4110	Randfontein Estates GM No R5
4114	Randfontein Estates GM No R6
4119	Randfontein Estates GM No R14 (second) *Cherrie.* Scrapped
4123	Randfontein Estates GM No R11 *Vivienne*
4125	Dunn's, hired to Durnacol. Later to Tweefontein Colliery No 2 *Margret*
4126	Tweefontein Colliery
4128	Randfontein Estates GM No R9 *Kathy*
4130	Randfontein Estates GM No R8
4133	Randfontein Estates GM No R10
4135	Randfontein Estates GM No R14 (third)
4136	Randfontein Estates GM No R12 *Barbara*
4168	Dunn's, hired to Durnacol. Later to Tweefontein Colliery No 1

The high mortality rate at Randfontein was due to some disastrous head-on collisions, caused by trying to operate a busy system under radio control. A proper signalling system has now been installed, with beneficial results.

Number series.

SAR Nos	Builder	Year
4051–75	Henschel	1952
4076–98	Beyer Peacock	1956
4099–4110	North British	1956
4111–20	North British	1958
4121–30	Beyer Peacock	1958
4131–40	North British	1958
4141–70	Henschel	1954

Class GO 4-8-2 + 2-8-4 Garratt

These locomotives were in all technical features identical to the GMA/M classes, but had smaller boilers and cylinders, bringing the axle load down to 13·4 tons, suitable for use over lighter track, on which they were never utilised. The real purpose behind this design was unclear, as they were never used over lines which could not take heavier power. Possibly their originally envisaged use had disappeared between the time of ordering and time of delivery.

At the opening period of this book, all were stationed along the North coast of Natal, at Stanger, Empangeni, and Gingindlovu. Here they worked the main line, then in course of electrification, often double-headed with a GMA/M or another GO, this being the only part of the SAR where double GOs were regularly operated. They also worked the line north to Gollel on the Swaziland border, and were the most powerful locomotives used on this line, for which their design features were finally justified shortly before withdrawal. Both the Eshowe and Nkwalini branches saw GOs used to replace the older GE and GEA Garratts, but on the Eshowe line their fire-throwing capabilities when climbing 1 in 30 gradients through sugar cane fields caused the GEAs to be returned until dieselisation of this and the other lines using GOs.

After displacement by diesels, the whole class was

Class G0 Garratt No 2577. Seen from the right angle, the smaller boiler, and taller, slimmer chimney are noticeably different from the larger GMA/M classes.

moved to De Aar where the locomotives spent seven years on the dump before being written-off abruptly early in 1984. Thus these modern and very effective locomotives spent only 22 years in service, being replaced by expensive diesels which were so feeble as to need using in multiple where a single GO sufficed, and whose consumption of imported fuel and imported spare parts became increasingly costly.

Distribution of this class was simple, thus:

1 April	1973	1974	1975	1976	1977 to 1983	1984
Natal	25	25	23	6	nil	nil
Staged	–	–	2	19	25	nil
Total	25	25	25	25	25	nil

Preservation and industrial. No GOs were sold to industry, but No 2576 has been retained for the National Railway Museum.

Number series.
Nos 2572–96, built by Henschel 1954.

Class H2 4–8–2T Ex-NGR Reid tank locomotives

These were the last tank engines to work on SAR, and were the survivors of 101 4–10–2Ts built by Dübs in 1901–03 for main line work on the NGR. Design features were typical of turn-of-century Great Britain, with plate frames, narrow firebox, and inside slide valves driven directly by Allan straight link motion. A peculiar feature derived perhaps from Ivatt's Atlantics on the English Great Northern Railway was the eccentric main crank pin, giving a 12in coupling rod throw combined with a 27in piston stroke.

After relegation from main line duties, most were rebuilt to 4–8–2T by the simple filleting of the trailing coupled axle, leaving a visible vacant horn gap. This eased passage on curves in sidings, and by then heavier rails permitted the increased axle load.

Although during their long lives the H2s worked fairly widely over SAR, the last ten survivors were

Class H2 4–8–2T No 243 shunting at Durban Wests in 1973, with the Bluff in the background.

concentrated at Greyville shed, Durban, where they worked on the pig-iron wharf at Durban Wests, and as Greyville shed pilot, plus any other odd shunting turn. The shed pilot lasted until the end of steam in Durban. Eight were running from April to October 1975, thence two until February 1976, the last survivor finishing in October that year.

Preservation. No 314 is preserved on Estcourt station and No 330 at the National Parks Board, Midmar Dam, both in Natal.

Industrial. Although many H2s were sold into industrial service, none was sold within the currency of this book, and the last industrial survivor, Tavistock Colliery No 1, only just outlasted the last SAR member.

119

Class S 0–8–0 No 369, sold to Grootvlei Proprietory Mines Ltd, becoming No 2 King Kong.

Class S 0–8–0 Built for SAR

Throughout SAR's history shunting has traditionally been the preserve of downgraded main line engines, and in view of the enormous amount of shunting carried out, the number of purpose-built shunters was remarkably low, amounting to only 151 locomotives on a railway whose steam stock reached a maximum of nearly 2,800. For all its new built shunting power, SAR cleaved to the American practice of total adhesion locomotives with separate tenders, rather than the European practice of tank engines.

The class S locomotives were the first SAR shunters, and being built by Henschel it is perhaps not surprising that they bore some similarities to the Prussian class G9H, although the SAR locomotives on the narrower gauge were the bigger engines!

The class S was very much a Western Transvaal type, being stationed mainly at Germiston, Kazerne, Krugersdorp, Springs, plus a solitary example at Volksrust. Capital and operating figures are as below:

Preservation. No 360 has been retained for the National Railway Museum, and No 372 preserved by the RSSA.

Industrial. Four have been sold into industrial service, all to Dunn's in 1977. Their brief industrial history is somewhat obscure, due to uncertain identities and removals from one site to another. The details below are believed to be correct.

SAR No	Disposal
362	To Apex Mines, Greenside, No 6
365	To Tweefontein United Colliery, later to Enyati Colliery
367	To Apex Mines, Greenside, No 5. Later to Grootvlei Proprietory Mines, Springs, *Big Mac*, No 3, later No 2
369	To Grootvlei Proprietory Mines, Springs, *King Kong*, No 2, later No 1

The two Apex locos were together on site during 1978, the remaining one was No 5 in 1979, and renumbered 6 in March 1981.

There was also one for a short time at Witbank Consolidated Colliery.

Year	1973	1974	1975	1976	1977	1978	1979	1980	1981	1982	1983	1984
Capital	14	14	14	14	13	12	2	1	1	1	–	–
Operating	14	14	13	13	–	–	–	–	–	–	–	–

Class S1 0–8–0 Built for SAR

The S1 were SAR's largest and finest shunting locomotives, with quite enormous shifting and accelerating ability. The first were built by SAR itself (the only steam locomotives it ever built) and were basically an S class chassis upon which was mounted a shortened 12AR boiler. British enthusiasts will be amazed to learn that this narrow gauge shunting engine is, in terms of tractive effort, adhesion weight, and grate area, approximately the same as the BR Class 9F 2–10–0.

In 1973 the locomotives were divided between Beaconsfield, Bloemfontein, Germiston, Kazerne, and Springs. A year later most were in the Western Transvaal at the same sheds, but two had gone to Witbank. Finally, in 1982 all were at Germiston and its sub-depot of Kazerne, after which they began to be withdrawn from service. A possible reason for

The SAR class S1 heavy shunter looked rather like a Garratt boiler balanced on eight wheels! No 3823 of these massive weight shifters is on the 'Sallies' (South African Lands and Exploration) transfer trip at Springs.

withdrawal was the closure of Koedoespoort works to steam repairs, a large lumbering 0–8–0 not being an ideal type for long-distance running to the nearest steam works at Bloemfontein.
Distribution was as shown below.

Preservation. No 374 *Voortrekker*, will probably be preserved.

Number series.
Nos 374–385. Built Salt River works, 1947.
Nos 3801–3825. Built North British, 1954.

Year	1973	1974	1975	1976	1977	1978	1979	1980	1981	1982	1983	1984	1985	1986	1987	1988
Capital	37	37	37	37	37	37	37	37	37	37	37	10	14	14	37	9
Operating																
Cape Northern	6	–	–	–	–	–	–	–	–	–	–	–	–	–	–	
Orange Free State	5	–	–	–	–	–	–	–	–	–	–	–	–	–	–	
West Transvaal	26	35	35	35	35	35	35	35	35	37	24	10	3	–	–	–
East Transvaal	–	2	2	2	2	2	2	2	2	–	–	–	–	–	–	–
Active	37	37	37	37	37	37	37	37	37	37	24	10	3	–	–	–
Staged	–	–	–	–	–	–	–	–	–	–	13	2	11	14	37	9

Class S2 No 3705 brand-new at Uitenhage Works.
W. King

The original unsuperheated class NGG11 locomotives were the first Garratts used on SAR. The two superheated versions, with piston valves, lasted until 1974, NG54 being shown at Humewood Road in 1967.

Class S2 0–8–0 Built for SAR

These small, snappy, terrier-like machines were built mainly for dock shunting, where they replaced various aged 4–6–0s, 4–8–0s and 4–8–2Ts. At the start of the period covered, 80 out of the 100 locomotives were stationed at Cape Town, Port Elizabeth or Durban, leaving but a score in the Transvaal for light general shunting. In Cape Town and Durban they were replaced by small diesel shunters of no greater capacity, but those at Port Elizabeth were replaced by older steam locomotives of larger capacity. In many ways, they are the victims of SAR's cockeyed accounting system, which counts costs 'per kilometre'. Since shunting engines do few kilometres, the low denominator of the equation gives a distorted 'high maintenance cost'. The new and expensive diesels which replaced them are similarly showing maintenance costs several times higher than much larger main line diesels, no doubt to the confusion of the accounting staff who are able to manipulate figures fed in to the system but who are totally ignorant as to what affects this input.

Of the non-dock shunting engines, it is worth recording that one S2 at Pretoria was painted blue for shunting Blue Train stock, until replaced by a 19D. The last S2 in service was the shed pilot at Waterval Boven, which has survived the rest of the class by several years.

Preservation. No 3775 has been retained for the National Railway Museum, and No 3778 has been preserved in working order at the Umgeni Steam Railway, Natal.

For some reason the 'staged' figures for this class are several years out of date from the true position, and the bulk of the class ceased work before the official figures indicate.

International. Four S2s were hired to Maputo in Moçambique for dock shunting.

Number series.
Nos 3701–3800. Built Krupp, 1952–53.

Year	1973	1974	1975	1976	1977	1978	1979	1980	1981	1982	1983	1984	1985	1986	1987	1988
Capital	100	100	100	100	100	100	100	100	100	100	99	2	4	2	6	4
Operating:																
Cape Western	23	23	23	23	31	31	31	31	31	–	–	–	–	–	–	–
Cape Midland	20	20	20	20	20	23	23	23	23	–	–	–	–	–	–	–
Natal	37	37	37	31	16	12	12	12	12	–	–	–	–	–	–	–
West Transvaal	13	13	13	13	12	11	11	11	8	–	–	–	–	–	–	–
East Transvaal	7	7	7	7	8	7	7	7	7	1	1	1	1	–	–	–
Staged	–	–	–	6	13	16	16	16	16	97	97	3	3	2	6	4
Hired Moçambique	–	–	–	–	–	–	–	–	3	–	–	–	–	–	–	–

Class NGG11 2–6–0 + 0–6–2 (2ft 0in gauge) Built new for SAR

The class NGG11 locomotives were the very first Garratts on SAR, three having been supplied in 1919. The first three were unsuperheated, and had slide valves—they were scrapped or sold before the currency of this book. However, two further examples were supplied in 1925, improved by the addition of superheaters and piston valves.

In 1973 both were at Humewood Road depot, Port Elizabeth, where their main duties were shunting, including transfer trips to and from the docks. However, the arrival of the class 91 narrow gauge diesels in 1973–74 resulted in a downgrade shuffle of steam power, and both were taken out of service in October 1974.

Preservation, and number series. Both locomotives have been preserved and details are as follows:

SAR No	Builder	Date	Preserved at
NG54	Beyer Peacock	1925	De Aar, for later National Museum
NG55	Beyer Peacock	1925	Weenan station

NG54 is currently being restored to working order in Bloemfontein works, after which it will be used at Port Elizabeth.

Class NGG13 2–6–2 + 2–6–2 (2ft 0in gauge)
Built new for SAR

This class of narrow gauge Garratt was greatly improved from the NGG11, having trailing wheels to each engine unit to improve the riding. Most dimensions were enlarged except, surprisingly, the grate area. The locomotives set the standard for future narrow gauge Garratts built over forty years. Whereas the earlier locomotives had outside plate frames and Belpaire fireboxes, the NGG13 had bar frames (also outside) and round-top fireboxes. All were built at a time when German builders were obtaining many orders from SAR.

In 1973 five of the class were allocated to the Cape Midland system, at Humewood Road, from whence they worked main line traffic on the Avontuur line. Seven were in Natal, of which five were nominally allocated to Mason's Mill shed, Pietermaritzburg, but actually divided between the Weenen and Mid-Illovo branches. The other pair were normally at Port Shepstone. After the arrival of diesels at Humewood Road, those on the Cape Midland were withdrawn, as were some of the Natal locomotives, replaced by NGG16 class.
Distribution was at 31 March:

Class NGG13 Garratt No 60, its number plate recording the class simply as 'NG G', is seen at Estcourt in October 1972.

Preservation.

SAR No	Disposal
NG49	Retained for the National Railway Museum, Umlaas Road.
NG50	Preserved in working order, Houston, Texas, USA.
NG60	Sold to owner at Schinznach, Switzerland.
NG77	At Brecon Mountain Railway, Wales.
NG79	Static preservation, Humansdorp.
NG80	Static preservation, Joubertina.
NG81	Static preservation, Patensie.
NG82	Sold to owner in Surrey, England.
NG83	Static preservation, Avontuur, later to Hanover, Germany.

Number series.

SAR Nos	Builder	Year
NG49–50	Hanomag	1928
NG58–60	Hanomag	1927
NG77–83	Hanomag	1928

Year	1973	1974	1975	1976	1977	1978	1979	1980	1981	1982	1983	1984	1985	1986	1987	1988
Cape Midland	5	5	5	–	–	–	–	–	–	–	–	–	–	–	–	–
Natal	7	7	6	6	6	6	6	6	6	6	5	3	3	–	–	–
Staged	–	–	–	–	–	–	–	–	–	–	–	2	2	4	3	3
Total	12	12	11	6	6	6	6	6	6	6	5	5	5	4	3	3

Class NG15 2–8–2 (2ft 0in gauge) Built new for SAR

This is the only non-Garratt type found today on SAR's 2ft 0in gauge lines. They were developed from the old class NG5, inherited from South West Africa, a curious 2–8–2 in which the leading carrying wheels were behind the cylinders. The NG15s have conventional cylinder layout, plus superheaters and piston valves, but in most dimensions remain similar to the original class.

The whole class was built for use in South West Africa, or Namibia as it is now called. The last five locomotives were officially purchased by the Tsumeb Corporation and leased to SAR from 1957 to 1961, when the new 3ft 6in gauge and diesel-operated line replaced the narrow gauge. The NG15 class locomotives were then transferred to the Avontuur line, where they have worked ever since, and which is now threatened with closure due to the negative, accountant-ridden, policies which beset SAR today.

One famous little train which they have always hauled is the Apple Express from Humewood Road to Loerie and back, run each Saturday out of the apple season, to cater for tourists. Today, except for the handful used on the Patensie branch, most of the locomotives are idle except during the apple harvest around Easter each year.

Twenty-one locomotives are still in capital stock, all classed as active until 1982. By March 1983 two were staged, and a year later eleven were officially staged, although some of these were brought out to work apple traffic.

Preservation. NG18 has been sold to an owner in Houston, Texas, while NG118 and 123 have been sold to Western Australia for a tourist line.

Building and number data.

SAR Nos	Builder	Year
NG17–19	Henschel	1931
NG117–119	Henschel	1938
NG120–124	Franco-Belge	1949
NG132–136	Franco-Belge	1952
NG144–148	Henschel	1957
	(ex-Tsumeb Corporation TC1–TC5)	

'Kalahari' 2–8–2 No NG121 basks in the afternoon sunshine as it turns on the Avontuur triangle.

Class NGG16 2–6–2 + 2–6–2 (2ft 0in gauge)
Built new for SAR

These are the most numerous of the 2ft 0in gauge locomotives today, and are indeed the only SAR steam class to remain intact as built. Technically they are a direct descendant from the NGG13 class, differing only in having roller bearings to the carrying axles. However, three varieties of tanks and bunkers are fitted, the older pre-war locomotives having the same riveted tanks, with large-radius tops, as on the NGG13. Later locomotives have welded tanks, with flat tops between the corner radii, and those built for Tsumeb Corporation had slightly more water capacity in the front tanks, while the rear bunker held more coal and no water, being designed to run with an auxiliary water wagon. The Tsumeb locomotives, built to work in South West Africa, were delivered directly to SAR, and were divided between the Umzinto, Port Shepstone, and Avontuur systems. The Hunslet Taylor batch were officially the last new Garratts built in the World, although in New South Wales, an AD60 Garratt was later assembled from spare parts to replace a similar locomotive which was beyond repair.

There was little external difference between class NGG13 and the earlier NGG16. No NG109 of the earlier series is seen at Joubertina early in 1968.

Six NGG16s were on the Cape Midland system on 31 March 1973, reduced to three a year later and nil by 1 July 1974. All were transferred to Natal, which today has the entire class. These later Garratts have not been used on the Weenen or Mid-Illovo branches, but operate entirely on the two systems running from Umzinto and Port Shepstone.

Building and number data.

SAR Nos	Builder	Year
NG85–88	Cockerill	1937
NG109–116	Beyer Peacock	1937
NG125–131	Beyer Peacock	1951
NG137–143	Beyer Peacock (ordered as Tsumeb Corporation TC6–TC12)	1958
NG149–156	Hunslet Taylor	1967–68

The Narrow Gauge in South Africa

As this book goes into print, substantial changes are being made to the 2ft 0in gauge lines in South Africa. On SAR itself, a narrow gauge museum complex is being set up at Humewood Road, Port Elizabeth, and this will house a wide selection of locomotives and rolling stock, many in working order. Trains will be operated regularly along a beachfront line under construction, together with the 'Apple Express' workings to Van Stadens. Steam operation is expected to continue on the Patensie branch for the foreseeable future, partly under the aegis of the new museum administration.

In Natal, all four narrow gauge systems were closed by SAR, and the Weenen and Mid-Illovo lines torn up. However, the Harding line has been privatised as the Alfred County Railway, initially operating a tourist train called the 'Banana Express', between Port Shepstone and Izotsha. The main project, however, was to reinstate freight traffic to Harding itself, and it was confidently expected that this could be effected competitively against road haulage which had been used since SAR closed the line. Since March 1989, two freights began running each way daily and this may be extended to the neighbouring Umzinto to Donnybrook section.

The Port Shepstone to Harding line winds through the Zululand escarpment, ever gaining height through the rolling hills. A class NGG bustles round a typical curve on this section.

LOCOMOTIVE DIMENSIONS

Class	Wheel arrangement	Coupled wheel dia ft	in	Cylinders in × in	Nominal valve dia in	Steam lap in	Valve travel in	Tractive effort @ 75% lb	@ 85% lb
1,1A	4–8–0	3	10	20½ × 24	slide	n.a.	n.a.	31,240	35,410
3R	4–8–2	3	10	21 × 24	slide	n.a.	n.a.	32,790	37,160
3BR	4–8–2	3	10	22 × 24	11	0·94	4·72	35,980	40,780
4AR	4–8–2	4	6	21½ × 28	11	1·19	5·88	32,360	36,670
11	2–8–2	4	0	20 × 26	10	1·0	4·75	30,870	34,990
12R	4–8–2	4	3	22½ × 26	11	0·94	4·69	36,780	41,680
12A/AR	4–8–2	4	3	24 × 26	12	0·94	5·00	41,840	47,420
14R	4–8–2	4	0	22 × 26	11	0·94	4·94	37,360	42,340
14CRB 14CR/CRM	4–8–2	4	0	22 × 26	11	0·94	6·00	35,400 37,360	40,110 42,340
15A 15AR	4–8–2	4	9	22 × 28	11	0·94	5·00	32,990 33,880	37,390 38,400
15BR	4–8–2	4	9	22 × 28	11	0·94	6·00	32,990	37,390
15CA/CB	4–8–2	5	0	24 × 28	11½	0·94	5·50	42,340	47,980
15E	4–8–2	5	0	24 × 28	8 inlet 9 exhaust	poppet		42,340	47,980
15F	4–8–2	5	0	24 × 28	11½	1·50	7·41	42,340	47,980
16R/CR	4–6–2	5	3	22 × 26	11	0·94	5·00	29,960	33,890
16DA	4–6–2	5	3	23 × 26	11½	0·94	5·36	33,570	38,040
16E	4–6–2	6	0	24 × 26	8 inlet 9 exhaust	poppet		35,280	39,980
19R 19B/BR	4–8–2	4	6	21 × 26	11	1·00	5·03	31,850	36,100
19A/AR	4–8–2	4	3	19½ × 26	11	1·00	5·03	29,080	32,960
19C	4–8–2	4	6	21 × 26	7 inlet 8 exhaust	poppet		31,850	36,100
19D	4–8–2	4	6	21 × 26	11	1·50	7·47	31,850	36,100
23	4–8–2	5	3	24 × 28	11½	1·50	7·50	43,200	48,960
24	2–8–4	4	3	19 × 26	10	1·50	7·00	27,600	31,290
25/NC	4–8–4	5	0	24 × 28	12	1·50	7·41	45,360	51,410
26	4–8–4	5	0	24 × 28	12	2·16	7·41	45,360	51,410
S	0–8–0	4	0	23¼ × 25	9	1·00	5·06	35,890	40,680
S1	0–8–0	4	0	23¼ × 25	9	1·00	5·06	38,010	43,080
S2	0–8–0	4	0	18 × 26	8	1·38	6·03	25,600	29,090
GCA	2–6–2 + 2–6–2	3	6¾	14 × 23	6½	1·00	4·47	28,470	32,270
GE(1/11)	2–8–2 + 2–8–2	3	10	18 × 24	8	1·00	4·31	45,640	51,730
GE(111)	2–8–2 + 2–8–2	3	10	19 × 24	8	1·00	4·31	50,850	57,630
GEA	4–8–2 + 2–8–4	4	0	18½ × 26	10	1·63	6·44	55,620	63,030
GF	4–6–2 + 2–6–4	4	6	16 × 26	8	1·19	5·53	34,200	38,770
GM	4–8–2 + 2–8–4	4	6	20½ × 26	11	1·63	6·56	60,700	68,800
GMA/M	4–8–2 + 2–8–4	4	6	20½ × 26	11	1·63	7·00	60,700	68,800
NG15	2–8–2	2	9⅞	15¾ × 17¾	6½	0·88	3·56	16,610	18,820
NGG13	2–6–2 + 2–6–2	2	9	12 × 16	5½	0·75	3·56	18,850	21,360
NGG16	2–6–2 + 2–6–2	2	9	12 × 16	5½	0·69	3·50	18,850	21,360
H2	4–8–2T	3	9	19 × 27	slide	n.a.	n.a.	28,430	32,220

LOCOMOTIVE WEIGHTS and typical TENDER CAPACITIES

Class	Locomotive weights (tons) Total	Adhesive	Max axle	Tenders (typical) Coal (tons)	Water (gal)	Weight	Weight Loco + Tender
1	70·55	56·45	14·70	8·75	3,675	n.a.	n.a.
3R	84·60	60·50	15·55	8·85	3,900	n.a.	n.a.
3BR	84·70	60·35	15·55	8·75	3,900	n.a.	n.a.
4AR	81·45	57·55	14·55	8·00	4,000	47·25	128·70
11	79·70	62·30	15·75	10·00	4,000	49·35	129·05
12R	91·60	64·90	16·70	12·00	6,000	66·00	157·60
12A	99·05	69·15	17·30	12·00	6,000	66·00	165·05
12AR	99·25	68·95	17·40	12·00	6,000	66·00	165·25
14R	90·40	63·60	16·50	10·00	4,600	52·35	142·75
14CRB	84·10	59·55	14·95	10·00	4,250	50·90	135·00
14CRM	90·55	65·40	16·75	10·00	4,250	50·90	141·55
15A	94·00	66·00	16·55	12·00	6,000	66·00	160·00
15AR	94·85	66·10	16·70	12·00	6,000	66·00	160·85
15BR	91·75	65·15	16·55	10·00	4,250	50·90	142·65
15CA/B	106·30	70·30	17·80	14·00	6,000	69·40	175·70
15E	109·00	73·40	18·60	14·00	6,000	69·40	178·40
15F	113·05	74·20	18·65	14·00	6,000	69·40	182·45
15F	113·30	74·50	18·75	14·00	5,620	69·40	182·75
16CR	82·75	52·80	17·70	12·00	6,000	66·00	148·75
16DA	90·55	57·20	19·10	14·00	6,000	69·40	159·95
16DAW	92·00	58·75	19·75	14·00	6,000	69·40	161·40
16E	97·75	59·75	20·95	14·00	6,000	69·40	167·15
19	79·45	53·05	13·45	10·00	4,250	51·05	130·50
19A	75·15	51·65	13·20	9·20	4,250	50·95	126·10

LOCOMOTIVE WEIGHTS and typical TENDER CAPACITIES

Class	*Locomotive weights (tons)* Total	Adhesive	Max axle	*Tenders (typical)* Coal (tons)	Water (gal)	Weight	Weight Loco + Tender
19B	78·70	51·20	12·95	10·00	4,600	52·35	131·05
19C	79·65	54·10	13·65	10·00	4,600	52·35	132·00
19D and 19C 'torpedo' tender				12.00	6,500	73·35	–
19D	81·10	54·05	13·60	10·00	4,600	52·35	133·45
23	111·10	72·50	18·70	18·00	9,500	107·70	218·80
24	72·90	45·20	11·50	9·00	4,520	56·55	129·45
25(C)	121·55	78·00	19·30	19·00	5,000	113·90	235·45
25NC	117·45	73·75	18·70	18·00	10,500	105·55	223·00
S	72·00	72·00	18·00	8·00	6,000	61·35	133·35
S1	74·40	74·40	19·90	11·00	6,000	65·65	140·05
S2	50·60	50·60	12·75	8·00	4,200	53·30	103·90
GCA	105·80	66·85	11·70	7·00	3,000	–	–
GE	148·40	103·50	13·45	9·00	4,600	–	–
GEA	183·90	114·80	15·00	10·00	5,600	–	–
GF	145·55	84·00	14·20	10·00	4,000	–	–
GM	174·30	115·10	15·00	10·00	1,600*	–	–
GMA	187·05	119·90	15·35	11·60	1,650*	–	–
GMAM	191·40	122·15	15·70	14·00	2,100*	–	–
GO	172·10	106·95	13·40	11·00	1,650*	–	–
H2	68·00	52·00	13·00	4·00	1,880	–	–
NGG13	61·65	41·00	6·90	4·00	1,825	–	–
NG15	36·60	26·40	6·80	5·50	2,860	31·20	67·80
NGG16	61·10	41·25	6·90	4·00	1,825	–	–

*plus auxiliary tank, 6,700 gallons, 51 tons

BOILER DIMENSIONS

Boiler Standard No	Used on classes	*Diameters* front inside ft	in	rear outside ft	in	Length between tube plates ft	in	Tubes no × diam in	Flues no × diam in	*Areas in sq ft* Grate	Firebox	tubes and flues	Super-heater	Pressure lb/sq in
1	24	5	0	5	4⅛	17	9	76 × 2½	24 × 5½	36	139	1497	380	200
1A	19AR/BR 19C 19D	5	0	5	4⅛	20	2	76 × 2½	24 × 5½	36	139	1839	390	200
2	3R/BR 4AR, 12R 14R/CR/ CRB/M	5	7½	6	0	19	4	87 × 2½	30 × 5½	37	142	2075	492	190
2A	15AR/BR	5	7½	6	0	21	8	87 × 2½	30 × 5½	37	142	2313	537	190
2B	16R/CR	5	7½	6	0	18	4	87 × 2½	30 × 5½	37	142	1978	472	190
3A	16E	6	2¼	6	7½	19	0½	136 × 2½	36 × 5½	63	232	2682	592	210
3B	15E/F 23	6	2¼	6	7½	22	6	136 × 2½	36 × 5½	63	232	3168	676	210/25
Non-standard boilers:														
–	1/1A	5	4½		–	12	1	325 × 2	none	34	132	2056	nil	190
–	11	5	1¾		–	18	0¼	121 × 2¼	21 × 5½	37	142	1829	331	190
–	12A	5	10½		–	18	0	159 × 2¼	24 × 5½	41	200	2308	515	190
–	12AR	6	0		–	19	4	119 × 2½	30 × 5½	41	164	2338	480	190
–	15A	5	4⅝		–	19	0	113 × 2¼	21 × 5½	40	192	1834	478	185
original	15CA/B	6	2¼		–	20	0½	143 × 2¼	30 × 5½	48	223	2554	716	200/210
reboilered	15CA/B	6	2¼		–	20	0½	117 × 2¼	34 × 5½	48	223	2361	570	200/210
normal	16D/DA	5	10¼		–	17	10⅝	181 × 2	30 × 5⅜	45	186	2453	593	205
wide firebox	16DA	5	10¼		–	17	10⅝	142 × 2¼	34 × 5½	60	194	2371	620	205
–	19, 19B	5	0		–	20	2	120 × 2¼	21 × 5½	37	140	2036	506	200
–	19A	4	10¼		–	20	0⅜	86 × 2¼	18 × 5½	36	140	1527	415	200
–	25/NC	6	4⅜	7	0	19	0	158 × 2½	40 × 5½	70	331	3059	630	225
–	26	6	4⅜	7	0	19	0	113 × 2½	50 × 5½	70	331	2773	788	225
–	GCA	5	2		–	11	3⅝	141 × 2	24 × 5½	34	163	1225	331	180
–	GE	6	9		–	11	8⅝	288 × 2	36 × 5½	52	202	2374	349	180
–	GEA	6	9		–	11	8⅝	282 × 2	36 × 5½	51	212	2328	470	200
–	GM	7	0	7	3	13	6½	255 × 2	50 × 5½	64	281	2785	778	200
–	GMA/M	6	11½	7	3	13	6½	282 × 2	50 × 5½	63	237	2974	636	200
–	GO	6	2¾		–	13	6½	241 × 2	36 × 5½	57	226	2399	546	200
–	H2	4	4⅞		–	10	4	287 × 1¾	none	21	135	1359	nil	175
–	NG15	3	11¾		–	13	1½	94 × 1¾	15 × 4¾	17	68	728	180	171
–	NGG13/16	4	7¾		–	9	3⅝	152 × 1¾	15 × 5½	20	82	839	149	180

CHAPTER 3

Steam Workshops and Depots

Steam Locomotive Workshops

Major locomotive workshops are an essential component of any large railway system, for it is within these that the ravages of wear and tear must be made good and, depending on the outlook of the chief mechanical engineer, design improvements effected. Since South African industry is a fairly recently developed phenomenon, it follows that with railways starting at various coastal points and pushing inland, the major workshops tended to be at or near the coast, where imported locomotives and rolling stock from overseas sources could be readily assembled and rendered operable.

Each works was originally devoted to the repair of rolling stock allocated to the relevant system, and has its own Mechanical Engineer who reports to the Chief Mechanical Engineer, whose office is in Pretoria. Each system also has a System Mechanical Engineer, responsible to the System Manager, and whose function is the day-to-day running maintenance of the system's rolling stock and other mechanical items such as dockside equipment.

In latter years, especially after steam locomotives started to decline, each workshop became a parent overhaul depot for certain locomotive classes, thus reducing stocks of jigs, tools, and spare parts, although sometimes necessitating long journeys for locomotives used at one end of the country but repaired at the other. Details of workshops relevant to this book are:

Cape Western System. Salt River Works, Cape Town, adjacent to Paarden Eiland running shed. This has been closed to steam overhauls since December 1983, but continues to overhaul 25NC class boilers for Bloemfontein. The last locomotive to be overhauled was class 25NC No 3481.
Cape Midland System. Uitenhage Workshops, currently in course of removal to new premises at Cuyler Manor. Steam overhauls ceased when this transfer was completed. The last locomotives to undergo repairs were 15AR and NG15.
Cape Eastern System. East London Workshops, closed to steam repairs in 1974. Last locomotive overhauled was class 15AR No 2020, which carries a suitable commemorative plate.
Cape Northern System. No separate workshops, but

a shop attached to Beaconsfield shed is sufficiently equipped to carry out intermediate repairs.
Natal System. Durban workshops was the main centre, closing to steam in 1972. The last locomotive overhauled was class GE No 2262, and in recent years the whole original works has been transferred to new premises at Bayhead.

Also in Natal was Pietermaritzburg works which closed down for locomotive repairs in 1985. The final steam classes overhauled were 15CA on 3ft 6in gauge, and NGG16 on the narrow gauge.
Orange Free State System. The workshops are at Bloemfontein which is very much a railway town, rather like Swindon was, or Crewe, despite its being the provincial capital and the judicial capital for the whole country. Apart from the workshops, Bloemfontein is also a major junction, with large locomotive depot and marshalling yards. In December 1983, of a total population numbering some 215,000 people, about 10,500 were railway workers who with their dependents amounted to 20 per cent of the city's inhabitants.

Bloemfontein is the last workshop on SAR to carry out heavy steam repairs, limited now to classes 15F and 25NC. At one stage overhauls were to continue into the 1990s, but a sudden change in motive power policy may alter this, and such work could cease in 1989.
Southern Transvaal System (formerly Western Transvaal). There is no steam workshop here, although Germiston has a major wagon works. Intermediate repairs are carried out at Germiston running shed.
Northern Transvaal System (formerly Eastern Transvaal). The main workshops are at Koedoespoort, East of Pretoria. These ceased steam repairs in 1978, the last locomotive overhauled being a 15CA.

Locomotive Depots

The locomotive depot or shed (*loods* in Afrikaans) invariably becomes a mecca for the enthusiast, whether he (or she) be interested in 'sitting duck' locomotive portraits, or finding out what engine is going where, and when, in order to determine which train to ride, or to chase for action photography. The shed itself always has a superb aura. A main line

shed is constantly filled with the sight and smell of smoke, steam, hot oil and coal dust, while massive machines ooze around as they perform their daily chores of taking on coal, water, sand and lubricants, or discharging ash and clinker. Fitters and boiler-makers move around fixing details ready for the next run, and the time office is always full of crews booking-on or off, and determining their next assignations. The larger shed also has a substantial repair shop, where wheel-less engines, dead as dinosaurs, can be seen propped up while essential moving components are in the machine shop, being made fit to perform another spell of arduous duty.

At the other end of the scale is the small country shed, home to perhaps one or two engines, which may seem totally empty and derelict when the engine(s) are out at work, enjoying a brief instant of action at the start and end of the day's run, interspersed by another long period where the faintly bubbling and sizzling locomotive is the only sign of life.

SAR's sheds are allocated on a system basis, and as usual there are main sheds with all major facilities, including repair shops, washout facilities etc., sub-sheds which house locomotives for branch lines or local work, and a host of minor engine termini, some with water and ash disposal points only. System by system, the sheds and main sub-sheds are listed below, * denoting that the depot has been closed since 1973.

Several locomotive depots boasted artistic entrances of the style shown at Glencoe, with a stylised class 12AR flanked by winged and wheeled springbok, suitable heraldic devices for a South African steam shed. Subsidiary notices are in Afrikaans, English, and Zulu.

Cape Western System
PAARDEN EILAND*, Caledon*, Dal Josefat*,
  Kalbaskraal*, Malmesbury*.
WORCESTER*, Hermon*, Wolsely*, Riversdale*.
TOUWSRIVIER*, Ladysmith*.
BEAUFORT WEST*, Hutchinson*.

Cape Northern System
BEACONSFIELD (Kimberley), Warrenton*,
Douglas*.
DE AAR.
KLERKSDORP, Coligny*.
MAFIKENG* (formerly Mafeking), Vryburg*.

Cape Midland System
SYDENHAM (Port Elizabeth)*, Alicedale,*,
Grahamstown*, Alexandra*.
ROSMEAD*.
MIDLANDIA* (Noupoort).
KLIPPLAAT*, Graaff Reinet*.
VOORBAAI* (Mossel Bay), George, Oudtshoorn*.
2ft 0in gauge
HUMEWOOD ROAD, Assegaibosch*,
  Humansdorp*, Loerie, Avontuur*.

Touwsrivier shed boasted the only really modern coaling plant on SAR, designed to accommodate the condensing 4–8–4s which would haul traffic to Beaufort West. By a supreme example of bureaucratic bungling it was commissioned just as the route was electrified – as a result, the expensive structure was used only by shunting engines and the locomotive for the sparse service to Ladysmith. In later days, with a class 15F on the shunt, the morning shift change produced the 'big main line' look, as designed for but never used.

(top right) Two class NGG13 Garratts sleep away a Sunday afternoon at Ixopo shed.

132

Cape Eastern System
EAST LONDON*, Kingwilliamstown*, Fort
  Beaufort*.
QUEENSTOWN*, Burgersdorp*, Sterkstroom*,
  Indwe*, Maclear*, Molteno*, Aliwal North*,
  Barkly East*.

Orange Free State System
BLOEMFONTEIN*, Springfontein*, Theunissen*,
Modderpoort*.
KROONSTAD, Bultfontein*, Bothaville*,
  Hennenman, Welkom*, Virginia, Vredefort*,
  Coalbrook (later Sasolburg)*.
BETHLEHEM, Harrismith*, Warden*, Frankfort*,
  Arlington*, Heilbron*.

Natal System
GREYVILLE (Durban)*, Bayhead*, Wests*, Kelso*,
  Port Shepstone*.
MASON'S MILL (Pietermaritzburg)*, Schroeders*,
  Dalton*, Greytown*, Donnybrook*, Franklin*,
  Underberg*, Richmond*, Estcourt*.
GLENCOE*, Newcastle*.
VRYHEID*.
STANGER*, Gingindhlovu*, Eshowe*.
EMPANGENI*, Nkwalini*, Mtubatuba*, Golela*.
2ft 0in gauge
PORT SHEPSTONE*, Harding*. (Privatised 1988)

UMZINTO*, Ixopo*.
Umlaas Road*, Estcourt*, Weenen*.

Western Transvaal (Southern Transvaal from April 1984)
GERMISTON, Kazerne*, Leeuhof, Potchefstroom,
  Klerksdorp.
SPRINGS, Balfour North*, Welgedag, Saaiwater,
  Vandyksdrift, Bethal*.
VOLKSRUST*, Standerton*, Vrede*, Bethal*,
  Balfour North*.

Note Both Balfour North and Bethal formerly
housed engines sub-shedded from Springs and
Volksrust.
MILLSITE* (Krugersdorp), Braamfontein*,
  Zeerust*, Potchefstroom.

Eastern Transvaal System (Northern Transvaal from April 1984)
CAPITAL PARK (Pretoria), Nylstroom*,
  Naboomspruit*, Rustenburg*, Thabazimbi*.
PIETERSBURG*, Tzaneen*, Phalaborwa*, Louis
  Trichardt*, Messina*.
WITBANK, Derwent*.
WATERVAL BOVEN*, Belfast*.
NELSPRUIT*, Sabie*, Barberton*, Komatipoort*.
BREYTEN*, Piet Retief*.

CHAPTER 4

The Friendly Neighbour

As the largest railway in Southern Africa, owning more locomotives than all the other countries combined, SAR has always been a reservoir from which neighbouring countries have drawn locomotives in time of need, either by hire or by outright purchase. During the period covered by this book, the railways of Rhodesia/Zimbabwe, Moçambique, Zambia, Zaïre, and Swaziland have been kept going by the hire of both steam and diesel locomotives from SAR, together with the hire of wagons. The reason behind this need for hired locomotives was the acquisition of 'political freedom' invariably leading to the Orwellian situation of everything for

Two ex-SAR locomotives at Matsapa, Swaziland. Classes 14R and 15AR in double harness was a combination never seen on SAR, where the two classes were rarely allocated to the same areas.

Party members and little or nothing for anybody else. This resulted in the emigration of most skilled artisans, and as locomotives and wagons are immune to political exhortation in lieu of proper maintenance, they simply refused to function. Details of the numerous locomotives hired are set out below, country by country.

Swaziland

The Swaziland Railway was initially run entirely by steam locomotives hired from Moçambique, with CFM locomotives from Lourenço Marques (now Maputo) running through to Sidvokodvo, from whence sub-shedded power continued up to Ka Dake and Matsapa. In 1973 all was steam, including a few workings by ex-SAR class 15BR which had been sold to CFM that year. The Frelimo party took over in

(above) *Withdrawal of steam from the Cape Eastern system has meant that Swaziland is the last place to see double-heading class 15ARs in regular service, even if they usually appear as scruffy as these two.*

(below) *Class 15E No 2886 rounds the curve from Mpopoma to Westgate in Bulawayo, while on hire to Rhodesia Railways, which eventually purchased the locomotive and renumbered it 886.* F. C. Butcher

(above) SAR class 12R No 1510 at Victoria Falls, en route to its brief hiring to Zambia Railways.   Nick Lera

(below) Class 15F No 3066 sits beside Rhodesian Railways class 20A Garratt in Bulawayo shed yard in 1979. The SAR locomotive is already disconnected and ready for towing back home.

In 1980 when much of Rhodesia Railways' heavy traffic was hauled by SAR Garratts, a class GMAM climbs through '404 Curve' south of Wankie, hauling coal for Bulawayo. Note the built-up bunker. F. C. Butcher

1976, and by the following year Moçambiquan steam power was a rapidly crumbling asset. From the end of 1977, locomotive hire was switched from CFM to SAR which initially hired class 14R, the first in November 1977 and reaching a peak of 16 locomotives in 1979. After heavy overhauls on this class were discontinued, the locomotives were from 1981 replaced by class 15AR, which continue to handle limited traffic in 1988, after monopolising the system until the new North–South link line, with diesel operation, was instituted.

Moçambique

This embattled country would have had a complete breakdown in its rail service had it not been for SAR which has hired both steam and diesel locomotives, repaired and operated the docks at Maputo, and overhauled the signalling system. At present, CFM diesels are being brought into SAR workshops for heavy repairs. Steam locomotives hired by SAR have been six 19D from December 1978 for eight months, and four S2 from December 1980, in each case for shunting at Maputo. In the longer term, GMA/M Garratts were on hire to the Beira system, up to a maximum of nine locomotives, from October 1980 to December 1983, some of them returning full of shell holes from guerrilla forces opposed to the communist regime. In addition, about ten to fifteen

CFM locomotives have been overhauled privately by Dunn's Locomotive works at Witbank, these including Montreal 4–8–2, Henschel 2–10–2, Baldwin 2–8–2T and Henschel 0–10–0T from Maputo, plus a solitary Belgian Garratt from Beira, which latter was towed dead right through Zimbabwe and Botswana eventually landing up at Mafeking totally unannounced!

Zambia

High oil prices coupled with an ever-ailing diesel fleet led management of ZR to experiment with steam in 1980. Ten class 12R were hired from SAR in March, but these dwindled to none six months later. Apparently nobody remembered how to work steam, and as it meant harder work than diesels, nobody was prepared to learn!

Rhodesia/Zimbabwe

This was SAR's biggest customer for steam hire and in 1970 RR hired six class 15E which were subsequently purchased, but then scrapped early

137

Helping the neighbours! Class 14R No 1921 is on loan to National Railways of Zimbabwe, and is shunting a coal load at Bulawayo in 1981.

in 1973 after a remarkably short period of service. Next were six class 15F, hired from November 1978 to mid 1979, although not popular with Rhodesian engine crews, who preferred Garratts. By then SAR had a surplus of GMAM Garratts, so from August 1979 to September 1981 these were hired in various quantities up to a peak of 22 locomotives. Although nominally the equal of a Rhodesian 20th class, and very similar dimensionally as shown in the table opposite, the SAR Garratts were very much heavier on coal, and despite having their bunkers temporarily increased in capacity by about two tons, tended to run short of coal especially on the long, 345km uphill climb from Thomson Junction to Bulawayo, invariably with loaded trains of coal or copper. The reason for heavy consumption was that SAR grates were designed for Witbank coal, while front ends were sharply draughted with a crude 'cross' (a sort of double 'jimmy') across the blastpipe cap. Modifications to suit Wankie coal

would probably have cured things without much effort, but as they remained SAR property this was not done, and resort made to reducing loads to those capable of haulage by the smaller RR 16A class.

During 1981 it was decided that better use could be obtained by returning the Garratts to SAR and hiring class 14R for use on the shunts at Bulawayo, this in turn releasing RR Garratts for main line work. This was then done, with 14Rs up to a maximum of 20 locomotives being hired from early 1981 to late 1982. An odd locomotive which appeared in the hire statistics was a solitary 19D, for a few months in 1978–89. Without confirmation, this is thought to be a Mafeking locomotive, hired to perform the Lobatsi shunt in Botswana, previously the duty of a RR 12th or 19th class 4–8–2. In March 1989, NRZ began negotiating the purchase of some twenty to thirty 25NC class from SAR.

Comparative dimensions – SAR GMAM, RR 20th and 16A classes

Class	Cylinders in × in	Wheels ft	in	Tractive effort @ 85%. lb	Grate area sq ft	Boiler diameter ft	in	Coal capacity tons	Locomotive weight tons
GMAM	20½ × 26	4	6	68,796	63·2	7	3	14*	242*
20A	20 × 26	4	3	69,333	63·1	7	3	14	225
16A	18½ × 24	4	0	58,183	49·6	6	6	11†	169+

* GMAM about 16 tons coal with built-up bunker. Weight including auxiliary water tank.
† 16A after rebuilding at RESCCO, probably 12 tons coal and 175 tons weight.

The following table details steam locomotive hirings by SAR over the interesting period from 1977 to 1984.

LOCOMOTIVES HIRED BY SAR TO NEIGHBOURING COUNTRIES

Railway	Loco Class	1977 11	12	1978 1	2	3	4-to-10	11	12	1979 1	2	3	4	5	6	7	8	9	10	11	12
SR	14R	6	10	11	11	13	14	14	14	14	14	16	16	16	16	16	16	16	16	16	16
CFM	19D	–	–	–	–	–	–	6	6	6	6	6	6	6	6	–	–	–	–	–	–
CFM	2S	–	–	–	–	–	–	–	–	–	–	–	–	–	–	–	–	–	–	–	–
CFM	GMAM	–	–	–	–	–	–	–	–	–	–	–	–	–	–	–	–	–	–	–	–
SNCZ	12R	–	–	–	–	–	–	–	–	–	–	–	–	–	–	–	–	–	–	–	–
RR/NRZ	15F	–	–	–	–	–	–	6	6	6	6	6	6	6	6	6	2	–	–	–	–
RR/NRZ	GMAM	–	–	–	–	–	–	–	–	–	–	–	–	–	–	–	12	12	12	12	12
RR/NRZ	19D	–	–	–	–	–	–	–	–	–	–	–	–	–	–	–	–	1	1	1	1

Railway	Loco Class	1980 1	2	3	4	5	6	7	8	9	10	11	12
SR	14R	16	16	16	15	15	15	15	14	14	12	12	12
CFM	19D	–	–	–	–	–	–	–	–	–	–	–	–
CFM	2S	–	–	–	–	–	–	–	–	–	–	–	4
CFM	GMAM	–	–	–	–	–	–	–	–	–	4	7	8
SNCZ	12R	–	–	10	10	?	7	1	–	–	–	–	–
RR/NRZ	15F	–	–	–	–	–	–	–	–	–	–	–	–
RR/NRZ	GMAM	21	21	22	22	22	22	22	22	22	17	12	12
RR/NRZ	19D	1	1	1	1	–	–	–	–	–	–	–	–

Railway	Loco Class	1981 1	2	3	4	5	6	7	8	9	10	11	12	1982 1	2	3	4	5	6	7	8	9	10	11	12
SR	14R	12	12	12	12	12	?	7	6	5	4	4	4	4	4	3	3	3	4	4	4	4	4	4	3
SR	15AR	–	–	–	–	3	?	11	12	13	14	14	14	14	14	15	15	15	14	14	14	14	14	14	15
CFM	GMAM	8	8	8	8	8	8	8	8	8	8	7	6	6	7	7	7	7	7	7	8	7	7	9	9
RR/NRZ	GMAM	12	12	6	6	6	6	6	6	4	–	–	–	–	–	–	–	–	–	–	–	–	–	–	–
NRZ	14R	–	–	6	6	11	?	14	14	14	18	20	20	20	20	14	14	14	14	14	10	9	9	4	–

Railway	Loco Class	1983 1	2	3	4	5	6	7	8	9	10	11	12	1984 1	2	3	4	5	6	7	8	9	10	11	12
SR	14R	3	3	1	1	–	–	–	–	–	–	–	–	–	–	–	–	–	–	–	–	–	–	–	–
SR	15AR	15	15	17	17	18	18	18	19	19	19	18	18	18	18	20	20	20	20	20	20	20	20	20	21
CFM	GMAM	8	8	6	6	4	4	4	4	4	4	3	1	–	–	–	–	–	–	–	–	–	–	–	–

CHAPTER 5

Economic Motive Power for Industry

For many years it has been normal practice for SAR and even its predecessors to sell outdated motive power for use by industrial organisations which in early days did not wish to invest too much capital on intermittently used services. However as industry (which in South Africa mainly meant mining) grew, these old second-hand machines, mainly ex-Natal 4–8–2Ts, were used more intensively. This intensive use provided the springboard for building new industrial locomotives, and based on the old Natal designs the North British Locomotive Company introduced lighter and heavier 4–8–2Ts for industrial use, the heavy version being developed into a 4–8–4T. Locomotive builders, both British and others, supplied surprisingly few industrials for South Africa, and NBL's success must be fairly placed on the old established firm of Reunert & Lenz, their agents in South Africa, and a well-respected organisation in both mining and railway fields.

By the period covered in this book North British had long closed down, but there was still a demand for steam locomotives in industry. For coal mining, steam is an obvious choice, since real fuel costs at pithead prices was negligible. Even other industries, sometimes far from coal mines, found steam economic due to the low capital costs of a second-hand ex-SAR locomotive, coupled to the very real economy of local coal versus imported diesel fuel. As the world oil crisis escalated, industry (unlike SAR) responded to the government's call to conserve oil by investing in steam power. In some cases steam was used to displace diesels, and in others where the purpose-built North British tank engines became inadequate for heavier loadings, they were replaced by older but more powerful ex-SAR machines.

At one stage the situation became very fluid and extremely interesting, with the cost of an ex-SAR locomotive being less than the overhaul of an existing locomotive, with the result that some organisations adopted the policy of 'run it into the ground and replace'. This situation seems now to have stabilised, and where more SAR locomotives are being offered for sale there are fewer buyers, perhaps due to high capital interest rates.

The procedure for purchasing locomotives (and other surplus items) from SAR is interesting. From time to time tenders for the purchase of surplus

material are issued by the Chief Stores Superintendent, and in the case of locomotives, it is the intending purchaser's responsibility to examine the locomotive(s) and offer accordingly.

Obviously, the highest offer for any locomotive is usually accepted and the tenderer is contractually bound to purchase any locomotive when his tender is accepted by SAR. From date of tender to SAR adjudication is usually about three months. Having been accepted, the successful tenderer has about a month's grace to remove what is now his property from SAR premises, after which he may be charged storage. To transport his new property from SAR to owner's premises the most convenient method is usually by rail, for which SAR charges. Since the locomotive is no longer SAR property, the purchaser must provide a representative to attend to lubrication and any problems arising, and since he is travelling on SAR he must also purchase a ticket! The latter detail may seem pettily bureaucratic, but is doubtless necessary for insurance purposes in the unlikely event of an accident, and is doubtless similar in other countries worldwide.

The subject of South African industrial steam is sufficiently extensive and complex to warrant a book on its own (or even several books) and within this tome coverage will be restricted to brief descriptions of the organisations which have purchased locomotives within the period starting 1973, plus a few details of what the locomotives do or did. Individual locomotive details will be found in Chapter 2. Many more locomotives will be found in South African industrial service, but these cannot be detailed here. A complete list of industrial locomotives is available from the RSSA, and is detailed in the bibliography.

The following pages briefly detail industrial sites as relevant to this book. Further details of the

(top right) *The old Enyati shed, by the mine, on a Sunday morning in 1976. The six locomotives are: first line – ex-SAR class GF and ex-RR 16th class Garratts; second line – ex-SAR class 12R; back line – ex-SAR class 14, class 1, and Baldwin 2–10–0T plus tender. Also present was a North British Locomotive Co industrial 4–8–4T.*

(below right) *In the glorious days when colliery locomotives were painted post office red, Greenside Colliery's class 1A leads the class 4AR as they approach Blackhill exchange yard with a load of coal. The photograph was dated 1975. The older class 1A locomotive remained in service at the time of writing.*

Apex Mines, Greenside Colliery, excelled in exotic double-headers. This 1978 scene shows class 1 No 2 ahead of lumbering class S No 5 in a combination unlikely to have ever occurred on SAR itself.

locomotives acquired from SAR during this period will be found under the locomotive class summary, Chapter 2. Purely industrial locomotives, and SAR locomotives acquired earlier will only be mentioned for continuity, but not in detail.

Transvaal

Apex Mines Ltd, Greenside Colliery, Blackhill

This coal mine ran a wonderful variety of motive power over its quite short trackage between the mine and Blackhill SAR exchange yard. In particular, up to about 1980 there were regular double-headers when a 39-wagon daily block load contract was conveyed in two trains of ten wagons (about 700 tonnes gross), followed by a 19-wagon double-header. The time of departure depended upon when SAR deigned to deliver the empties. As from 1973,

the locomotive population has comprised two class 1, bought somewhat earlier, two class 4AR, two class S, two 14R, a 19A, and very briefly a GEA on hire from Dunn's. Virtually any combination of these classes could be seen double-headed and the number of locomotives on the premises at one time varied from four to six. They are still in service.

Blesbok Colliery, Broodsnyersplaas

This colliery had been dieselised, and ran trains with a diesel locomotive fore-and-aft, but maintained steam as standby power. There was a GCA Garratt from the 1960s, and in 1974 the colliery bought a 3BR. Steam action was very rare.

Butakon Limited

A private address in a residential area, which bought class 19A No 710 for hire or resale.

Delmas Colliery, Hawerklip

At the end of a long electrified branch from Delmas

station, steam work was confined to shunting. This was one of the sites which worked on the principle of 'run 'em into the ground and get another!' In 1973, the colliery had three old 7 class 4–8–0s which had been there since opening, then there was a class 1, two 16CR Pacifics very briefly, an industrial 4–8–4T for a while, and dieselisation in 1978. Having run through some relatively modern steam power, the company then bought an ancient 13 class 4–8–0, umpteenth-hand from half the collieries in the Transvaal, to cover the days when the diesel's battery went flat, or whatever!

Douglas Colliery, Vandyksdrift

At one time, one of the really spectacular colliery workings, as loads had to be lifted from the hollow containing the mine before rolling down to the SAR interchange. The final steam purchased was a class GM Garratt, which ran with an old Mallet tender, working in conjunction with two industrial 12As and an ex-Rhodesian 16th class Garratt or two. Just before the oil crisis worsened in 1977, the colliery ordered two large main line type diesels and has been lumbered with them ever since.

Fluor (SA) Pty Ltd

This was the American-based company which masterminded the Sasol II petrol from coal project. The mine came into operation before the main plant, and some of the early coal production was railed out. Two ex-SAR engines, a 19A and a 19B, shunted the sidings for a year or two.

Grootvlei Proprietory Mines Ltd (GVPM), Strubenvale, near Springs

A gold mining outfit with a main line about 8km long, connecting the reduction plant with shafts 3 and 6. One of its specialities is the operation of a passenger train for mine workers, at shift change. At the opening of the period covered, the mines had three ex-SAR class A 4–8–2T. These were replaced by two class S in the late 1970s, then at the end of 1983 were bought two class 14R, all ex-SAR. In the

A pair of ex main line locomotives at 3 shaft of Grootvlei Gold Mine, Springs, in 1983. On the left is veteran class 8DW 4–8–0 Puffing Duggie, 79 years old and ready to retire, while on the right class S 0–8–0 Big Mac trundles past the headgear.

*Two ex-SAR locomotives at work at the Grootvlei
Proprietory Mines, Springs, in 1984. Class S Big Mac
loads hoppers under the bins at 3 shaft, while an
unnumbered class 14R handles the midday passenger
working for 6 shaft.*

interim, they also had a class 8 about fifth-hand through the mining 'flea market' for locomotives. A pleasant mine, with green locomotives running through bluegum trees, and past a vlei (swamp) where flamingo may be seen.

New Largo Colliery, Arbor

Most of the output from this mine goes straight into the adjacent power station by conveyor belt. However, from time to time the colliery gets contracts to rail coal out, and the odd tank engine which potters around Monday to Friday may be supplemented by another. In 1977 a class 19B was acquired from SAR, but today this merely takes its turn with the other potterers. Rail traffic ceased in 1987, and locomotives were transferred to Enyati.

Randfontein Estates Gold Mines (Pty) Ltd

This really is the big steam success story of the 1970s and 1980s. By far the largest mining group in the West Rand, the whole system was moribund in the late 1960s. Railway lines ran everywhere, mine

Randfontein's class 14R with smoke deflectors, No R6, arrives at Millsite with an internal service wagon, plus an ex-SAR passenger coach en route to the RSSA collection.

headgear cluttered the horizon in all directions, and a large stock of tank engines sat in the locomotive shed, perhaps one being steamed for stores train duty, Mondays to Fridays. One man of the old breed, Cooke, reckoned that there was gold, not so much 'in them thar hills', but in the valley, and diligent prospecting proved he was right.

A new railway line was built from near the old shaft at SD32, down to the new Cooke shaft, and as the old tank engines were not really adequate for this longer run, three class 15BR and a class 1 were bought from SAR. Due to a collision between the class 1 and a 15BR, each was replaced by another of the same class. In 1979–80, a pair of class 14R locomotives was bought to cope with increasing traffic. During the 1980s two further shafts were built, Cooke 2 and Cooke 3, the original becoming Cooke 1, while a new reduction plant at Cooke was also commissioned. By then, there was a main line some 25km long from Cooke 3 to Millsite. At an earlier stage, two diesels bought by the same mining

Randfontein's class 1 No R4, resplendent in blue livery, heads a load of reef from SD32 shaft to Millsite reduction plant in 1983.

group for another mine were foisted on Randfontein, which found them slow, expensive, and unreliable. For the new line to Cooke 3, electrification was considered, but at half a million Rand per kilometre, plus locomotives, this was also rejected. In the event, Garratts were the answer, plenty of GMAMs being available; these were capable of hauling 1,200 tonnes up the ruling gradient of about 1 in 65. Five GMAMs were purchased early in 1983, followed by another four later in the year. The first was steamed in April 1983. A further shaft, the Doornkop section, is due to commence operations about 1986–87, and three further GMAMs have been acquired for this, making twelve in all!

Until 1983, the standard REGM livery was Caledonian blue, with yellow lettering and lining, but from late that year a new livery of maroon and gold was adopted: only three Garratts and all the 'straight' locomotives were outshopped in blue. However, the livery has now reverted to blue, with black and gold lining. This is an exciting industrial line with at least six locomotives in steam, and the best place to see in South Africa to see large Garratts at work.

Rustenburg Platinum Mines (Pty) Ltd

In the same mining group (JCI) as Randfontein, RPM had the largest mining railway in the Transvaal until the latest Randfontein extensions. RPM started off with a 2ft 0in gauge system powered by a mixture of new and SAR locomotives, but by the late 1960s this was virtually dieselised. The 3ft 6in system originally had but a single steam locomotive, and to all intents and purposes was dieselised from the outset, using a comparatively large fleet of these.

Came the oil crisis, and a pair of industrial 4–8–4Ts was bought in 1974, followed by two class 15CB in 1977. These proved so effective and economical that it was decided to change over from diesel to steam traction and in 1979 eight class 14R locomotives were bought from SAR. Arriving all at the same time, they have tended to wear out together, and at the time of writing traffic is hauled mainly by the two class 15CB locomotives plus a couple of 15CAs hired from SAR, with one or two 14Rs in steam. Various liveries have been tried: a light blue 15CB, later painted dark blue, a maroon 14R, and another of the class in GWR green, but crews prefer black, which shows up dirt less obviously!

South African Coal Estates, Landau 3 Colliery, Blackhill

During the currency of this book, the mine had a fine selection of locomotives painted in dark maroon, an industrial 12A, an ex-Rhodesian Railways 16th class Garratt, and in the 1970s an ex-SAR class 3BR. These alternated on the daily workings until about 1980, when all the mine's production was sent by conveyor belt to a new rail loader for export traffic. Rail traffic has now ceased, but all three locomotives have been preserved at the RSSA Witbank centre.

South Witbank Coal Mines Ltd, Saaiwater

At the beginning of this saga, the mine was operated with three ex-SAR class 11, but from 1978 these were gradually replaced by 15CBs, also ex-SAR. During 1984, having apparently appointed a mine engineer who thought that locomotives never needed any sort of maintenance, these big engines fell apart, and were temporarily replaced by two machines from Tavistock Colliery—another 15CB and one of its old class 11s! All three 15CB are again in good working order.

The first class GMAM in service at Randfontein Estates Gold Mines Ltd was No R9. It is seen here in 1983 resplendent in new blue and yellow livery, easing a load of new orange hoppers through the loading silo at Cooke 1 shaft.

Springbok Colliery, Main section, Vandyksdrift

Mainly worked by purely industrial locomotives, in 1981 the company acquired a class 3BR from Blesbok colliery. Locomotives are kept in immaculate condition, and today the 3BR alternates with an industrial 12A. The mine itself has now closed.

Springbok Colliery, Hope section

Mainly worked by industrial tank engines, the colliery had a class 3BR for a very short period in the 1970s. Rail services have now been replaced by a conveyor belt system.

Tavistock Collieries, Saaiwater

This mine originally ran its 'main line' to Kromklip station, but about 1980 this was replaced by a brand-new railway curving the opposite direction to Saaiwater marshalling yard, taking in on the way

(top left) *A class 15CB of South Witbank Colliery starting out from the reception sidings, soon after acquisition from SAR. Shortly after, the locomotive was turned to face the 'wrong way' for photography, as preferred by the line's personnel.*

(below left) *Air brakes for the mines! Standardisation is ignored against the accountants' false economies as two class 15CB locomotives at Tavistock Colliery each sports a different make of air-brake pump!*

Two former SAR locomotives hard at work at Tweefontein United Collieries in the Witbank coalfield. The first is a class 15BR of Canadian build, while the second is a Swiss-built class 19A.

the new Arthur Taylor shaft, originally known as Tavistock 2. In the same JCI group as South Witbank, Tavistock originally had three class H2 tank engines, one of which was the last in industrial service. The collieries then had some hand-me-downs from South Witbank, an 8DW and some 11 class, but in 1979 and 1983 built up a stock of class 15CB heavy locomotives. About 1982, two 11s and two 15CBs were fitted with air brakes, using proper steam donkey pumps bought from the USA and Germany. Until largely replaced by class 15CB locomotives, the mine offered the spectacle of class 11 locomotives nearly eighty years old running on a brand-new railway built to modern standards. Furthermore, these ancient Mikados, running like sewing machines, blasted uphill with empties with crisp, clear exhaust notes, sounding as though they were taking their trains to the end of Africa!

Transvaal Navigation Collieries, Bezuidenhoutsrust

A complex system which shared a main line with New Clydesdale and Albion Collieries, each with its own locomotives. A wide variety of motive power has been used over the years, but relevant to this book was a class GM Garratt, used for a short period in 1977, and a GF acquired in 1975 and still on the premises. About 1980 the collieries bought some diesels, and seem to feel obliged to use them, but retain a couple of steam locomotives for when the fan belts break. . . .

Tweefontein United Collieries, Minaar

A complex system comprising the old mines at Coalville, now closed, Waterpan section, and the new section opened about 1980, complete with a new railway connection. The company went from one extreme of the most decrepit locomotive shed in South Africa (which eventually fell down, perhaps with a slight push), to a brand-new 1980s locomotive shed, the best in industry at the time.

Many ex-SAR locomotives have hauled coal from the pits, some as permanent inhabitants and some hired from Dunn's. Until about 1981–82 double-heading was usual, with just about any combination of the variegated locomotive stock. Earlier, there were two 15BR, a 19A, and a 19AR. Dunn's then weighed-in at odd times, with a GF, a GM, and an S class, and in later years has run to an industrial 12A, an ex SAR 12R, two 15CB, and today four GMAM Garratts, all air-braked, plus another three in course of purchase.

Witbank Colliery Ltd

Regular motive power on this mine has been standard industrial 4–8–2T and 12A class. From time to time, when some of its own locomotives have

been under overhaul, the mine has hired a GEA Garratt from Dunn's often double-heading it with one of its own engines. A diesel was eventually obtained from SAR and steam work ceased. The locomotive shed area has been donated to the RSSA Witbank group, who use it as its preservation centre.

Witbank Consolidated Coal Mines Ltd

At the beginning of the review period, this mine was worked by three old SAR class 7 4–8–0s. The old shaft closed, and was replaced by a new pit, but two of the old class 7s moved, too, into a brand-new lean-to shed. For a while, Dunn's hired out a class S while the mine's latest acquisition is a domeless 19AR, ex-Tweefontein. Later, the two class 7 were donated to the RSSA preservation group, and a 12R, 12A, and a 15CB were transferred from Tweefontein.

Cape Province
Middelplaas Manganese Mines

This operation in the far northern Cape near Sishen bought three class 12R from SAR in 1980, fitting them with air brakes with proper steam donkey pumps, the first such equipment in South Africa. The mine is now worked out, but the locomotives are being transferred to Sishen.

Natal
Durban Navigation Collieries (Durnacol), Dannhauser

In 1973 this mine relied on several class 1 locomotives, some having been purchased when the mine opened in 1939, and which were later supplemented by others hired from Dunn's. When the new shaft was opened in the 1970s, including an extended main line and the introduction of a passenger service, a further assortment of locomotives appeared on site, including an ex-RR 16th class Garratt with Giesl ejector, two class 16CR used mainly on the passenger trains, a class 15E (which would hardly work as the mine could not set the poppet valves) and then a GM Garratt which ran

(top right) *Erupting from Wolwekrans Colliery, blue-painted Witbank Colliery class 12A No 5 leads a class GEA hired from Dunn's with a heavy load bound initially for the SAR exchange sidings at Witbank.*

(below right) *An 'international' link-up on the Enyati Railway as the former SAR (originally NGR) class 1 4–8–0 No 2 double-heads with maroon Garratt, ex Rhodesian Railways 16th class No 618, at the Nek with empties for Enyati.*

Glimpse of a possible future – two Garratts haul coal in air-braked wagons. This photograph shows class GF locomotives on the Enyati Railway in Natal, but much larger and more modern Garratts are possible.

Export coal for Richard's Bay, in air-braked wagons, climbs from the Nek on the Enyati Railway, with class GF Garratts fore and aft. The tin-roofed cage behind the bunker contains the anachronism of all time – a diesel-powered air compressor on a steam locomotive!

with an old class 1 tender in lieu of the standard water tank. The final and more reliable steam power were two class 15CB and a pair of GMAM, all hired from Dunn's. In 1984 ISCOR, owners of the mine, which produced coking coal, failed to agree with Dunn's on renewal of the hire contract, and drafted in surplus diesels from its steelworks. The two GMAM went to Tweefontein, and the 15CB to JCI mines, but the others will probably be scrapped.

The Enyati Railway

This remarkable concern is unique in South Africa as it is a *railway*, not just a line serving a mine. It serves several mines, not all owned by the same mining houses, and has about 16 miles of main and branch lines running through the most beautiful mountainous countryside.

In 1973 it operated about eight locomotives (plus several more derelicts), and the photograph on page 141 shows seven of these, all different, outside the shed on a Sunday morning. During the 1970s, traffic increased dramatically, and the locomotive stock which included ex-SAR classes G, 1, and the only class 14 which escaped rebuilding to a 14R, was expanded to include a 12R, an S, two GEA, and no fewer than ten GFs, not all at one time. Other exotica included ex-Rhodesian Railways Garratts, and ten-coupled Baldwins. Dunn's took over the old locomotive shed as a workshop, relegating running locomotives to Boomlager yard, where later a

modern mechanical coaling plant was erected. Air-braked wagons for export coal traffic resulted in a weird diesel-driven compressor contraption on the GFs, and the same unit mounted on old tender frames for other classes. Anything could happen in Enyati operation, and triple-headed Garratts have been photographed on more than one occasion. The most extraordinary combination seen by the author, which assembled so quickly that there was no time to move to a suitable photographic location, was an uphill departure from *the nek* comprising a GF, seven air-braked wagons, two more GFs, and seven or eight vacuum-braked wagons, truly a train with dual braking! At the intermediate water stop, after which a good photographic location was available, the cavalcade broke itself into one air-braked and one vacuum-braked trains, and a light engine.

Today, the contract with Dunn's has terminated, and surplus locomotives obtained from New Largo. At least one of Dunn's GF Garratts has been purchased, and more may follow, including two GMAMs.

South African Industrial Cellulose Corporation's route is the original south coast main line along the Umkomaas River, now by-passed by a shorter route over a longer bridge. In 1980 class 8 No 5 heads a short load to the plant.

On a winter weekend in 1982 two class GEAs were working at Vryheid Coronation Colliery! Here on the Sunday morning the mine's green-painted No 5 hauls from the shed its black-liveried sister from Enyati, on loan.

Gledhow-Chakerskraal Sugar Estates Ltd, Chakaskraal

The only Natal sugar estate remaining with steam haulage, and only for the short trip from the mill to the SAR exchange yard. Two class 1, and two class 19A were purchased in the 1970s, with one of each remaining today.

Natal Cambrian Collieries Ltd, Ballangeich section

After a variety of ex-SAR and industrial tank engines, this is now operating with two class 14Rs.

Newcastle Platberg Collieries, Elandslaagte

A small mine of many locomotives, believing firmly in the principle of running them into the ground and replacing with the cheapest available at the time. Apart from industrial types, the mine has seen class G 4–8–2Ts, class 7 4–8–0s, and in 1976 a big splash out into two 19As and the solitary 19R. All have

been scrapped, including now the mine itself. Rather the opposite of the old Rolls-Royce story, this mine replaced its locomotives when the ashpan was full!

South African Industrial Cellulose Corporation (SAICCOR), Umkomaas

Once dieselised from the outset, this operation was foremost in de-dieselising using four ex-SAR class 8 4–8–0s, somewhat before this survey. As the 4–8–0s wore out, one was donated to RSSA and another exchanged with SAR for a 19D, of which there are now four on site. These are now being painted a splendid blue livery.

Umgala Colliery, Utrecht

Another mine with a rapid turnround of loco-motives, this time due to an unfortunate habit of letting trains run away on the gradient down to the

155

SAR station, resulting in overturning on the final sharp curve, or high speed collisions in the yard! A pair of class 6 4–6–0s was soon thus disposed of, and three class 10C acquired about 1970 had all gone by 1977. Other ex-SAR types used since were a class 11 and a 16DA, and after trying out the odd industrial tank engine, the colliery now has a class 3BR. By the time this book is published, there will likely be further changes.

Vryheid Coronation Colliery Ltd

A large complex, including a coking plant, which by industrial standards has taken quite good care of its motive power. Four North British tank locomotives form the backbone of the steam power, working the coking plant and doing other jobs. The main line to Hlobane station has seen a couple of GCAs and an ex-RR 16th Garratt, after which a diesel was obtained. As this aged and became less reliable, the mine bought two GEAs, which in turn were used as diesel stand-bys. The original livery was blue, but locomotives are now green.

Vryheid Railway Coal and Iron Co, Hlobane Colliery

Once an extensive system including coking plants, this has now contracted to just a colliery. Ex-SAR locomotives used have been a GCA, a class 1, a 16DA, and a 15E which probably never ran. The mine was later dieselised, but about 1982 a class GF hired from Enyati was seen in use.

Orange Free State

The industrial locomotive population in the Orange Free State has seen a remarkable *volte face* since the oil crisis. Before 1970, industry comprised mainly the gold mines centred on Welkom, and these tended to use either standard North British tank engines, or diesels. Came the oil crisis, and many steam locomotives were bought from SAR, in some cases steam nearly eighty years old replacing relatively new diesels. In general, this ancient steam has proved useful, economical, and popular with staff, such that there seems no tendency to reintroduce diesels.

Free State Geduld Mines Ltd, Welkom

Uses four ex-SAR locomotives out of a fleet of eight. Each locomotive is different – one each of classes 3BR, 11, 19B and 19BR.

Loraine Gold Mines Ltd, Allanridge

Apart from tank engines, it has the last active class 10CR, and a pair of 19B, all maintained immaculately.

President Brandt Gold Mining Co Ltd, Welkom

Still uses some diesels, but has no less than four class 11 on the books, the largest collection of this class remaining.

St Helena Gold Mines Ltd, Welkom

Uses no less than five ex-SAR class 16CR Pacifics, the only ones in regular service.

Western Holdings Ltd, Holdings Division, Welkom

Various tank engines, a diesel, and one each classes 3BR and 11, in maroon livery, may be seen on these premises.

Western Holdings Ltd, Saaiplaas Division (formerly Free State Saaiplaas) near Virginia

This mine opened only in 1981, but is worked by a class 3BR and a class 11.

Welkom Division

Dieselised, but has a class 1A and a 12R, neither of which has been used.

Freegold North Division

This is an amalgamation of Western Holdings and Freestate Geduld, and locomotives have been renumbered into one series.

Twice daily, at 05.00 and 17.00, the shunters in Cape Town's Table Bay harbour assembled and ran coupled together to Paarden Eiland shed for coal, water, and crew change. Within the hour they were back on duty. Here seven class S2 0–8–0s trundle off at the end of the day shift, just before the end of steam in 1981.

CHAPTER 6

Regional Roundup

The foregoing parts of the book have dealt with the development of South African steam power, plus fuller details of the classes which survived in SAR service from 1973 to time of writing. As mentioned elsewhere, South Africa is a steam photographer's paradise, with locomotives working hard, often through spectacular scenery, and in superb sunshine. This section of the book, divided into the operating systems used by SAR, is devoted to a pictorial record of steam at work, area by area.

In the last year of steam shunting in Cape Town docks class S2 0–8–0 No 3717 backs through the maze of dockside tracks with the massif of Table Mountain looming in the background.

Cape Western System

Based on Cape Town, and extending to De Aar to the North and Riversdale to the East, this system in 1973 used steam on the main line from Beaufort West to De Aar, from Worcester to Riversdale, and on many branches to Bitterfontein, Saldanha, Bredasdorp, Protem, Porterville, Franschhoek, Prince Albert Hamlet, and Ladysmith. All have been dieselised except the Ladysmith branch, closed due to extensive flood damage. A few steam locomotives were kept at Cape Town for specials, while the last active steam in regular service was for shunting at Touwsrivier and Beaufort West. The region is now devoid of steam.

(above) *In Table Bay harbour class S2 No 3717 shunts refrigerator trucks against the backdrop of the Lion's Head pinnacle, while workers walk towards the Taiwanese trawler Che Hong No 12.*

(below) *1975 was the last year when the export apples from Elgin were steam hauled over Sir Lowry's Pass on the first stage of their journey to the cooling plant at Cape Town docks. Early in the morning a class 14CRB assists a class GEA in this final spectacular operation.*

(top right) *The only train on the line on Sundays was the 06.30 mixed from Riversdale to Worcester, which took ten hours for the 240km journey. Soon after departure it is seen here in 1977 climbing through the rugged country typical of the area.*

(below right) *Fruit for Cape Town docks en route from Elgin in 1975 with yet another standard team of class 14CRB plus GEA Garratt.* Christine Durrant

(above) *The RSSA Cape Town Branch organised a special train from Cape Town to the spectacular Ceres line in 1978. Descending the rocky gorge on the return trip class 19C No 2439 makes the whole thing worthwhile.*

(top left) *A poppet-value class 19C north of Moorreesburg on the Malmesbury–Bitterfontein line.*

(below left) *The branch from Touwsrivier to Ladysmith was washed-out in the floods of 1981, and closed as the light traffic did not warrant re-opening. Although finally worked by class 24 locomotives, the 1969 shot of a class 7 evokes nostalgia.*

(below) *The last southbound steam-hauled Orange Express leaves Orange River station January 1984 behind condenser 4–8–4 No 3511. A rebuilt condenser stands on the main line with a freight, ready to follow the passenger train.* Christine Durrant

Cape Northern System

This comprises the main line from De Aar via Kimberley to Ramathlabama, just past Mafikeng, the border with Botswana, and to Klerksdorp on the main line to Johannesburg, as were the branches from Coligny to Welverdiend and Klerksdorp, and other lines to the West of the above. Currently, main line steam operates from De Aar to Kimberley, and from Kimberley into the Orange Free State, this being programmed to continue until the mid 1990s. Mainline steam nearly ended in 1988, as a result of company policy, but a worldwide outcry against this caused a change of heart, and about half a dozen steam trains are scheduled to run daily at least until the beginning of the 1990s.

Another main line to retain steam until 1988 was that from Warrenton through Vryburg to Mafikeng (formerly Mafeking until respelled in the Tswana idiom). This was for many years a 19D line, after which GMAM Garratts were used for several years until finally replaced by 25NC on heavier track. An interesting working during 1987 was the operation of steam across the border from Mafikeng into Botswana, due to a political dispute preventing Botswanan and Zimbabwean engine crews from driving their diesels south. Two 25NCs were allocated to this service, with their own crews, one being painted blue! This operation has now ceased.

(left) *Attacking a gradient between Orange River and De Aar, No 3428* Selma *leads a rebuilt condenser on about 40 loads of coal as they charge south in the winter of 1981.*

(top right) *Class 25NC No 3436, brilliantly turned out with red wheels and white trim, races through Poupan on the last steam-hauled northbound Orange Express in January 1984.* Christine Durrant

(below right) *Following hard on the heels of No 2644 class GMAM Garratt No 4 blasts out of Vryburg with about 40 Zambian empties on their long return trek from Port Elizabeth to the copper belt.*

(below) *Early on a winter morning at the famous station of Kraankuil a pair of 'worshonde' (sausage dogs) – the name given to rebuilt condensers – speeds uphill on the Kimberley to De Aar main line.*

(above) *Wardale-modified class 19D No 2644 leaving Vryburg with the 12.45pm passenger train to Mafikeng in 1983. In the background may be seen another class 19D locomotive shunting in the stockyard sidings. Brewing-up in the station is the Garratt that was to follow ten minutes later.*

(below) *Every afternoon two or three coal trains of 38 to 40 bogie trucks would be seen blasting out of Orange River station behind pairs of 4–8–4s, in this case of the original class 25NC.*

Cape Midland System

A complex system of lines radiating from Port Elizabeth North to Noupoort and De Aar, plus all connecting links and branches West to Riversdale. East of the Port Elizabeth main line it also includes the branches to Alexandria and Port Alfred. In 1973 all except the main line was steam operated, and in the mid to late 1970s it was perhaps the most photographed part of South Africa as the services, though sparse, ran through some of the most spectacular scenery. There was also the added attraction of the 2ft 0in gauge branch to Avontuur. For performance enthusiasts there was the tightly-timed suburban service from Port Elizabeth to Uitenhage, where locomotives nearly 70 years old accelerated up to a mile a minute with 11-coach trains! Until 1987 steam locomotives still worked the short section from Voorbaai to Mossel Bay, the branches to Knysna, Alexandria, Port Alfred and Somerset East, plus the extensive shunting at Port

Normal practice on SAR is to run the smaller locomotive in front when double-heading. Unusual then is this northbound freight approaching Koloniesplaas heading for the Lootsberg Pass, with a class 19D locomotive heading a class 24.

Elizabeth. Futher steam locomotives shunt at Noupoort, and a little runs on the 2ft 0in line—the Patensie branch and the tourist Apple Express. Many of these branches are threatened with closure, SAR having acquired a sort of 'Van der Beeching' who thinks that railways should not run trains! After 1988 steam will probably be limited to a daily train between George and Knysna, plus the 2ft 0in gauge section which will include the official SAR narrow gauge operating museum, as described on p. 204.

After being refurbished for an enthusiasts' excursion, Sydenham's class 12R No 1505 was kept in good order by working an evening train daily from Port Elizabeth to Uitenhage until services were dieselised in mid-1983. Here it is seen approaching Swartkops on this duty.

(top left) *An 11-coach suburban train from Port Elizabeth to Uitenhage accelerates out of Swartkops Junction in July 1982, to provide a classic photograph in the last winter of steam operation.*

(below left) *Steam suburban services in latter-day South Africa tended to be single-track affairs of rather rural character. However, the inner section on the Port Elizabeth service was in the true suburban style as typified by this scene at Sydenham station, complete with signalbox and overbridge. The train, however is rural, being the local passenger from Kirkwood, hauled by class 19D No 3339, in its usual immaculate condition.*

(above) *The Toorwater River pierces the Groot Swartberg mountain range through a rugged defile which is followed by the Klipplaat–Oudtshoorn railway. Here the 1979 Sunset Limited southbound threads its way along the narrow ledge cut to take the railway line.*

(below) *The Oudtshoorn area was noted for ostrich breeding and for brilliantly clean class 19D locomotives on the line to Klipplaat. Here the two are combined near Le Roux, with a spectacular mountain backdrop.*

(top left) *The Indian Ocean rolls in inexorably to the coastline breached by the Kaaimans River, bridged by the George to Knysna line. Trundling across during Easter 1984 is SAR's special tourist train, billed as 'Tootsie' and hauled by a class 24 locomotive.*

(below left) *High above the Malgaaten River a class GMAM Garratt heads towards Mossel Bay in December 1978 with the daily Port Elizabeth to Cape Town passenger train. Within a year this service had been dieselised, using two diesels instead of a single steam locomotive.* Christine Durrant

(above) *Downhill, cab-first, Garratts are not normally considered the best photographic material. However this class GMAM, clearly articulating, rounding the curve into Topping in late 1978 shows that such a shot can be highly satisfying.* Christine Durrant

(above) *Crossing the Hankey River at the village of that name a pair of class NG15 locomotives hustles a train of empties for fruit loading at Patensie in 1982.*

(below) *A favourite train for photographers was the Sunday morning working from Stormberg to Rosmead – a portion of the East London to Cape Town train. Dawn*

breaking near Teebus in winter nearly almost guaranteed two class 15AR locomotives in clear freezing weather.

(right) *It is well below zero at Schoombee as a pair of class 15AR locomotives returning on a freight after working the Sunday morning passenger train set off to their home depot of Burgersdorp after taking water.*

Cape Eastern System

Very much a branch line empire comprising a main line from East London to Springfontein, cross-country connections from Blaney to Cookhouse, and from Stormberg to Rosmead, plus a whole host of branches to Seymour, Umtata (Transkei), Qamata (Transkei), Tarkastad, Maclear, Jamestown, Hofmeyr, and Barkly East. Although the main line was dieselised in the 1960s, most of it saw a few steam workings until 1982, due to the movements of locomotives to and from the central steam depot at Queenstown. The Umtata and Cookhouse lines both went diesel about 1970, but the remainder remained steam until 1980–82. Again, a well-known enthusiasts' paradise, due to the Maclear and Rosmead lines traversing some of the coldest areas in South Africa, where one might photograph a double-header in snow. The Barkly East branch was noted for its eight Andes-type reverses, built to change height rapidly. This system was fully dieselised from 1982.

(top left) *The barren Karoo stretches apparently for ever as a domeless class 19D locomotive heads a goods train towards Sterkstroom on a winter afternoon.*

(above) *At the end of term for the local schools the daily passenger train from Maclear to Sterkstroom was strengthened and double-headed. The last such working was in July 1982, when standard and domeless class 19D locomotives are seen crossing the Tsomo River at Cala Road.*

(below left) *Approaching Clark's siding, a domeless 'Dolly' climbs through bleak and rugged country with the daily (except Sundays) Maclear to Sterkstroom passenger train.*

(below) *The wind is travelling faster than the train as a class 24 2–8–4 battles along the bleak winter landscape with the Jamestown mixed train.*

Orange Free State System

This system is more-or-less self-explanatory, and has a main line from Noupoort in the South to Vereeniging in the North. Westwards it runs to Beaconsfield, near Kimberley, and to Orkney, near Klerksdorp. Towards Natal the Orange Free State system stops at Harrismith, while the secondary line from Bethlehem towards Johannesburg is OFS until Vaaldraai, just north of Villiers, and in the middle of nowhere. In 1973 the line Vereeniging–Kroonstad–Harrismith was in electric operation, while Bethlehem to Vaaldraai (and Balfour) was diesel. Otherwise, it was virtually all steam, except that some diesels wandered from the south into Bloemfontein. Slowly but steadily this has changed, with electrification extending south to Bloem-

fontein, plus the branch to Welkom. Bloemfontein south to Noupoort and to Aliwal North are diesel operated, as are several branches. Main line steam runs from Bethlehem to Bloemfontein, and to a lesser extent today from Bloemfontein to Kimberley. Branches remaining steam worked today are those to Winburg and Glen Harmony. Two rather special branches have become diesel, that to Koffiefontein, where through Fauresmith the train ran along the main street, and that to Maseru (Lesotho, formerly Basutoland), an international branch line.

For many years the most scenic route for 25NC 4–8–4 has been that from Bethlehem to Bloemfontein, especially the northern section, but this was diesel-ised, with greatly reduced service, in 1987. Steam remains for the present between Bloemfontein and Kimberley, but for how long is difficult to forecast.

(top left) *The morning freight from Barkly East to Aliwal North crosses the Kraai River near the station of that name. A well-cleaned class 19D is the motive power in this 1978 shot.*

(below left) *In order to gain height from the river gorge, the freight train from Barkly East to Aliwal North traverses a zig-zag known as reverses 7 and 8. It is seen reversing up the middle section from lower and upper lines, both clear in the photograph.*

(below) *Approaching the final summit between Barnea and Bethlehem, a well-cleaned class 15F heads the overnight passenger train from Bloemfontein in 1973.*

(left) *Winter in the Free State. Temperatures below zero are not uncommon in winter in this part of South Africa, and normally cloudless skies co-operate to provide optimum photographic opportunities, as with this class 25NC on a Kimberley–Bloemfontein freight train.*

(above) *Wide and standard firebox class 16DA locomotives in 1972, on the daily Bethlehem–Bloemfontein passenger train, approaching Meynell siding.*

(below) *Late afternoon sees the 'Bombela' departing from Barnea en route for Bethlehem behind a super pair of class 25NC 4–8–4s. The double-headed working occurred at long weekends, when many miners and others returned to their native Lesotho.*

(above) *The tiny cabs on narrow gauge Garratts were extremely hot in summer, hence the seats on the handrails, which could be swivelled outside to catch the breeze! Class NGG13 No 60, at Broomcliffe in 1972 with the daily Weenen to Estcourt mixed train, shows this feature in use.*

(top left) *Well-cleaned class 25NC No 3420 opens-up round the sharp S-bend before climbing to Owanty siding with the Bethlehem–Bloemfontein passenger train on a winter Saturday in 1979.*

(below left) *The Bethlehem–Ficksburg local passenger train, strengthened at long weekends, is usually double-headed with two class 25NC locomotives. Easter 1982 saw the train with the unusual combination of class 15F plus 25NC.*

(below) *Zulu lads cavort in a tributary of the Tugela River in October 1972 as class 19A No 691 crosses on the daily mixed train from Estcourt to Bergville.*

Natal System

Again self-explanatory, the extent of this system comprised all lines in the province, connecting at Harrismith with the Orange Free State system, and at Volksrust and Piet Retief with the Western and Eastern Transvaal systems respectively. In 1973 the main line from Durban to Volksrust and the inner suburban lines round Durban were electrified, but otherwise all was steam except the Ladysmith–Harrismith connection, also electric. Natal was the home of most of SAR's Garratts, being very heavily graded. It was the last province to see diesels, but also the first province to eliminate steam entirely, except for the 2ft 0in gauge branches of which there were four. All four of these branches have been closed by SAR, but one has been reopened under private enterprise, as described on p. 204.

(top left) *In its final years the branch from Newcastle to Utrecht was very 'main line' in character, with double 15Fs hauling long trains to and from the coalfields. Just before dieselisation, two of these locomotives condense exhaust into a cool winter morning, leaving Newcastle.*

(below left) *The Sunday afternoon local passenger train*

from Empangeni to Gollel, hauled by class GO Garratt No 2594, utilises the new formation for the Richard's Bay coal line, quite close to Nseleni, in 1975.

(above) *Heading a rake of cane empties, a class GO Garratt assaults a 1 in 30 gradient near Dikinyana on the Eshowe branch.* Christine Durrant

(top left) *The last regular steam working between Pietermaritzburg and Donnybrook was the Sundays only (returning Mondays) local freight train, which exchanged locomotives due for washout. A class GCA for the Underberg branch and a class GF Donnybrook shunter team up through the majestic Zululand scenery towards the end of steam.*

(below left) *A rare double-header at Cramond in 1972. Class GO No 2590 on transfer from the Transkei to Natal's North Coast is 'borrowed' by Mason's Mill shed, and is seen piloting a class GMA/M Garratt with a train on the Greytown line. Note the built-up bunker.*

(above) *Class H2 4–8–2T No 243 potters along the waterside at Durban Wests, hauling three of the special wagons holding containers for loading pig-iron. Behind is 'The Bluff' and its whaling station, now closed.*

(below) *On a sunny Sunday afternoon with typically summer cloud brewing in the background, a class 24 2–8–4 departs from Dunottar with a Springs–Nigel local passenger train (see Western Transvaal).*

Western Transvaal System, now Southern Transvaal

The new title describes the extent of this system accurately, it having a main east–west axis from Witbank to Mafikeng and lines south thereof extending north to Pretoria. Connections are made with the Cape Northern at Klerksdorp and Mafikeng, with the Orange Free State system at Vereeniging and Grootvlei, Natal at Volksrust, and the Northern Transvaal at Magaliesburg, Pretoria, Witbank, Broodsnyersplaas, and Breyten. By 1973 nearly all the main lines in this system were electrified, and only the Springs–Breyten line ran main line steam passenger trains, while the Springs–Nigel suburban service was steam. Today, the Breyten line is all diesel, and the Nigel line is electrified right through to Kaydale. Branches dieselised as late as 1983 were Volksrust to Bethal, and Standerton to Vrede, while Balfour–Grootvlei–Redan remains steam worked. Despite this gloomy picture, this is the steamiest system in South Africa today, having large numbers of locomotives which spend their lives shunting or performing trip working, mainly under the wires, but also on the numerous non-electrified sidings serving local industry in the Witwatersrand.

(top left) *The Heidelburg–Springs local freight train is silhouetted against a summer sky, with a class 15AR locomotive at the front.*

(below left) *On a freezing morning in 1981 a class 15F hustles a Bethal–Springs freight near Leslie.*

(above) The Abattoir train – 1. *Springs' only class S1 peels away from the main goods yard at the head of a rake for the higher level yard adjacent to the local abattoir.*

(below) The Abattoir train – 2. *Pushing hard behind, a classes S and S2 combination give all that they have got to get the load from Springs yard to the abattoir sidings.*

(top left) *The 1984 drought badly hit the little Transvaal town of Volksrust. Luckily there was a good supply of water for locomotives at Wakkerstroom on the Bethal line, and for a few weeks double-headed class 19Ds hauled water trains to the stricken township. Some busybody then decided that it was incongruous to haul water by steam trains, and the line was promptly dieselised. The next drought there will see no relief from Wakkerstroom as the water supplies there are redundant and disused.*

(below left) *Just east of Largo on the Springs–Breyton line a good summer's rain fills a depression against which the* next winter a class 15F has been caught with its silhouette in reflection on a cool morning.

(above) *Hendrie's 16th classes of Pacific, although designed for the best passenger trains, were sturdy and sure-footed machines, thus ensuring their survival on all sorts of local goods and passenger turns. Class 16CR No 828 is seen on a pick-up goods to Nigel, circa 1975.*

(below) *The 17-coach overnight passenger train from Lourenço Marques (now Maputo) to Pretoria rolls into the defile of Panpoort behind a pair of class 15CA 4–8–2s during the summer of 1973–4 (see Eastern Transvaal).*

Eastern Transvaal System, now Northern Transvaal

The old 'Eastern' nomenclature of this system dates back to the days when (as the NZASM) it connected Pretoria with Lourenço Marques, in Moçambique. Today it comprises the east–west axis from the Moçambique border at Komatipoort to Middelwit, with all northerly branches therefrom. It encompasses the Barberton branch, the line south from Machadodorp to Breyten and Piet Retief, including the Lothair branch, and the two connecting lines to Broodsnyersplaas. From Pretoria, it also extends west to Magaliesburg. In 1973, the main lines Pretoria–Witbank, and Pietersburg north to Beit Bridge and Tzaneen were steam worked, together with the Thabazimbi line and most branches. The Lothair and Vaalwater were the last branches using steam, both with double-headed 24 class, and the Magaliesburg branch now only sees special passenger workings. The Cullinan passenger service was steam worked until discontinued in 1983, while the Carolina pick-up train from Waterval Boven was steam until 1984, often with double-headed GMAMs. Steam shunting remains around Pretoria and Witbank.

(top left) *The Breyton–Lothair train is piloted as far as Voorslag by a class GMAM Garratt running nominally 'light engine' before taking a load south to Piet Retief. This working was to utilise line capacity in this once congested area.*

(below left) *In 1981 The Locomotive Club of Great Britain, touring South Africa and Zimbabwe, requested steam haulage from Beit Bridge to Pretoria. SAR obligingly marshalled its coaches (plus one for the RSSA) on the front of a freight train hauled by a pair of immaculate class 15Fs.*

(above) *During the drought-ridden winter of 1983 a pair of class 24 2–8–4s starts out from Burgerspan water stop with about 40 empty timber trucks for loading at Lothair. Note the extra water tank coupled to each locomotive.*

(below) *Due to tunnels the deviated line to Tzaneen would 'be diesel from the outset.' Just to disprove this, a class 15F hauls the daily passenger train from Pietersburg over the new bridge across a valley now flooded.*

(above) *A colourful encounter at Witbank. Class 26 No 3450 The Red Devil is seen on the ashpit after a test run from Pretoria, in juxtaposition with blue class 12A from Witbank Colliery.*

(below) *During the interim period on the Roossenekal branch, a class 15F leads a class GMAM on an early morning ore train for the Highveld steelworks.* Christine Durrant

(above) *Class 15CA No 2850 leaves Cullinan, discovery site of the world-famous Cullinan Diamond, with a local passenger train to Pretoria in 1980.*

(below) *Before eventual electrification, increasing traffic on the Derwent to Roossenekal branch demanded steadily heavier motive power, in pairs, from light to heavy 4–8–2s and finally to double Garratts. In an intermediate stage we see a combination of class 15CA plus GMAM Garratt leaving the ore terminus.*

CHAPTER 7

The Wardale Locomotives

After the last new GMAM had been placed in service, steam traction, although handling most of the traffic, was almost totally neglected for two decades inasmuch that modifications and experimental work were reduced to a minimum. The largest modification was the conversion of most 25 class 4–8–4s from condensing to non-condensing, carried out in the 1970s.

About this time D. Wardale entered the service of SAR, itself quite remarkable as the railways tended to make things difficult for non-South Africans to enter the service. Wardale had a British degree in mechanical engineering, and his BR railway service was on the Southern Region after the end of steam. Nevertheless, he was an ardent modern steam protagonist, and a disciple of L. D. Porta in Argentina. The world oil crisis gave him the excuse to do something about improving steam traction, despite the operating department's myopic infatuation with diesel traction, Even so, the turgidity of executive indecision was such that his first conversion was done 'unofficially'.

The Cape Northern system had to rely on class 19D for the important link between Warrenton and Mafikeng, where these smallish branch line engines had no reserve of power at all. This section of Cecil Rhodes' original pioneer Cape to Cairo railway was still laid with light track, yet had to cope with import and export traffic to and from Rhodesia and further North.

Class 19D No 2644, a particularly poor-steaming member of the class, was selected for conversion, which included a double Lempor exhaust. The Lempor was a Porta variant on the Lemâitre, and had a four-jet blastpipe, with extended petticoats to provide truer ejector proportions. The smokebox was extended 300mm to accommodate the arrangement. Steam flow in the cylinders was slightly improved by streamlining the edges of piston valves, which each had an additional valve ring to reduce leakage.

The firebox was modified to the gas-producer system, wherein principal combustion is effected using secondary air introduced above the firebed, through ducts in the firebox sides. Primary air was restricted through dampers and re-design of the grate. Turbulence in the firebox was created by steam jets, and formation of clinker inhibited by introducing exhaust steam under the grate. Sanding was improved, and de-sanding jets were fitted to clean the rails after the locomotive had passed.

Results with No 2644 were encouraging, with coal savings and increased output in the order of 20

The first Wardale conversion, class 19D No 2644, with original small tender but with the addition of very ugly smoke deflectors, heads an early test train from Beaconsfield to Belmont.

to 25 per cent, and sanction was given for modifying one of the 25NC class, representing the best and most modern motive power on SAR's steam roster. No 3450 was chosen for the experiment, the choice being dictated by which locomotive was about to undergo overhaul at Salt River works, at the time when all new components had been manufactured. The principal features in No 3450 were as follows:

1. Gas-producer firebox as in No 2644, but mechanically stoked as in the other members of the class. Secondary air ducts in the firebox sides and crown were made from sections of flue tubes, and welded-in. The grate was slightly lowered as far as practicable, to increase firebox volume. Pinhole firebars were limited to 5% airspace, restricting primary air supply to about 30–50% of the combustion air. As with No 2644, some steam from exhaust and auxiliaries was led under the grate to cool the fire and thus inhibit clinkering. Some of the secondary air ducts carried live steam jets to create turbulence in the combustion space.

2. A larger superheater was applied, using a GMAM header casting, which with a little modification could be fitted in. The number of elements was thus increased from 40 to 50, and calculated final steam temperatures raised from 380°C maximum on a class 25NC to 450°C on the rebuild.

3. The smokebox was lengthened to include the new exhaust arrangement and the self-cleaning plates made aerodynamically smooth to lessen gas resistance. An asbestos rope seal was fitted to the door to reduce leakage.

4. The exhaust fitted is the double Lempor, this being the Porta modification of the Lemâitre system. A Kordina was included in the exhaust manifold, this acting as an ejector, the exhaust from one cylinder reducing the back pressure on the opposite one. A curved vane mixed exhaust flows and created a swirl. As there are two chimneys, the exhaust flow was divided accordingly. Each blastpipe has a cluster of four nozzles of oval de Laval section. The two chimneys were angled fore and aft to a 'V' configuration in order to obtain maximum possible length for maximum ejector action effectiveness.

5. A weighted baffle was fitted across the lower six rows of small tubes, the purpose of which was the diversion of more gases through the superheater when working at less than maximum output. At full output, the strong draught raised the baffle, allowing more gases to pass through the small tubes.

6. A feedwater heater, utilising exhaust steam, was fitted between the two chimneys, within the space left by their 'V' formation. The construction was a tubular heat exchanger,

and the heated feed at high temperature was mixed with direct feed from the tender. Feed was by a turbo pump gleaned from a converted condenser class 25, plus one injector for direct feed when necessary. In practice, the turbo pump not only proved troublesome, but was also unable to cope with the much higher feed rates of the rebuild, and later twin pumps were supplied.

7. New steampipes were fitted, straighter than the originals, to improve steam flow and reduce pressure drop. Axial bellows were fitted to take up expansion strains.

8. New steamchests of larger size were fitted by cutting out the old and welding in new sections. A single through valve liner was fitted, carrying both piston valve heads, making valve fitting and withdrawal easier, and reducing likelihood of valve ring distortion during fitting. Helical passages on the outside of the liners were fed with saturated steam, thereby cooling the surface of the liner in contact with superheated steam. This facilitated improved lubrication at the higher temperatures attained, without materially affecting steam temperature to cylinders. The liners were cast in perlitic chromium iron for high wear resistance, and ports enlarged, and radiused for optimum steam flow.

9. New piston valves were fitted having steam lap increased from 38mm to 55mm (1½in to 2·36in), with 4mm exhaust lap. The valves themselves were bevelled to make the valve rings control admission. Maximum cut-off was reduced from 80% to 65% in full forward gear, and Herdner starting valves fitted to try and overcome starting difficulties at restricted cut-off. Twelve narrow rings were fitted to each valve head to minimise steam leakage, and bronze bearing surfaces applied to lessen wear, while an articulated valve spindle was fitted to take up any misalignment between valve and crosshead. The only changes needed to the valve gear were lengthening the combination lever between valve crosshead and radius rod pins, and increasing length of eccentric rod to compensate for this.

10. The piston heads were modified with welded-on fillers to decrease clearance volume. Koppers rings were substituted by three narrow perlitic iron rings, and again, bronze bearing surfaces applied. The cylinder liners were also cast in perlitic chromium iron.

11. Several improvements were made to the valve and cylinder lubrication systems, and both valve and piston packings improved with multiple metallic packings closed by garter springs, and allowed float to take up any wear in the pistons, valves, slide bars, etc.

12. Air sanding was fitted, using diesel locomotive

193

No 3450 **The Red Devil** *approaches Fouriesburg in 1981 with the daily passenger train from Bethlehem to Bloemfontein. The locomotive is still in its original condition with small smoke deflectors and air-sanding belt compressor driven from a pulley on the left trailing coupled wheel.*

components. As no air-brake equipment was fitted, the air supply was at first generated by a small pump belt-driven from a pulley mounted on the left trailing coupled wheel. In practice, the belt often broke, and later the pump was chain-driven from the mechanical stoker motor.

13. The external appearance of the locomotive was altered substantially by raising the running plates and fitting small smoke deflectors of similar shape to a Czechoslovakian class 498.1, which the rebuild strikingly resembled. In addition, it was given a distinctive red livery, with a single silver line along the running plate valence continued through the cab and tender. Officially named *L. D. Porta* after the Argentine engineer who inspired Wardale, the staff at Salt River dubbed it the 'Red Devil', a nickname by which it is generally known. New number plates were cast, bearing the legend 'class 26'. No recognition of this is made in SAR's staid monthly and annual locomotive returns, although the General Manager's annual report for 1980–81 includes a colour illustration captioned 'class 26'.

Into Service

No 3450 was outshopped from Salt River in February 1981 and after a few running-in trips in the Cape Town area was despatched to Pretoria for initial load tests, the CME's office being in that city. Test runs were made on the Pretoria–Witbank line, abounding in 1 in 50 gradients, and providing a real test of the locomotive's capabilities and weaknesses. There was no doubt about the power output —it climbed those 1 in 50 banks with barely reduced speed, as though they hardly existed! The major weakness was fundamental, and nothing to do with Wardale unless he can be accused of putting a quart of power into a pint pot. No, the fundamental weakness was the wheel arrangement, with far too little of the locomotive's total weight available for adhesion.

It is interesting at this stage to review some SAR eight-coupled types, and see how basic power output climbed without a commensurate increment in adhesion.

The two earlier 4–8–2 types with short lap valves and correspondingly high maximum cut-offs, are quite sure-footed. The class 15F is somewhat less so, but quite acceptable under SAR weather conditions, while the class 25NC is noted as being on the slippery side. The class 26, which dimensionally is still a 25NC, is a poor performer at starting or low speeds on steep gradients. The limited maximum cut-off means wider regulator openings, and these cause it

| Year | Class | Type | Tractive effort (lb @ 75% pressure) | Weight tons | | Adhesion factor |
				locomotive	adhesion	
1920	12A	4–8–2	41,840	99·05	69·15	3·70
1925	15CB	4–8–2	42,440	103·35	68·15	3·60
1935	15F	4–8–2	42,340	108·6	71·70	3·78
1953	25NC	4–8–4	45,360	117·45	74·25	3·68

to slip. Neither the Herdner valve nor the air sanding seemed able to overcome these problems, and on its first run to Witbank, a signal stop on a 1 in 50 gradient resulted in great struggles to restart, with about twenty minutes' delay. Wardale was well aware of this and at one time proposed converting the locomotive to a 4–8–2, to provide perhaps an extra 7 or 8 tons adhesion, but time did not permit the conversion. Valve gear alterations to increase travel and maximum cut-off were also too extensive for such a 'one-man' locomotive rebuild.

On the other hand, whereas the cylinders were too large for the adhesion at starting, they were too small for the most efficient development of full output at speed, the locomotive having to be driven at nearly full forward gear (about 60% cut-off) for full power! What was really needed was a totally new chassis, with ten coupled wheels, higher axle load, larger cylinders, and redesigned valve gear, but this was totally beyond the time and resources available.

However, what the locomotive *did* prove was that one could take what is considered a locomotive of relatively modern design, and improve it out of all recognition in both power output and fuel economy. Dynamometer car tests carried out between No 3450 and unconverted No 3428 during October 1983 were summarised by Wardale in the *Continental Railway Journal* No 57 for Spring 1984 and showed that at 75kph (the highest speed tested), the unmodified locomotive produced only 3,037ihp, which might rise to 3,200ihp at 100kph. By comparison, No 3450 produced 4,492ihp at 75kph using 52% cut-off; extrapolation of the curve produces an estimate of 5,030ihp at 100kph—all this from a narrow gauge, simple-expansion locomotive weighing less than 120 tons without tender. It is worth comparing this with Chapelon's class 240P of 1940 which, at 112 tons locomotive weight plus higher boiler pressure, compounding, poppet valves *et al*, produced 4,000 metric horsepower at 110kph and a maximum of 4,172 at 134kph.

The higher power of No 3450 can be accounted for partly by better use of the steam generated, also by the higher steaming rates attained. Whereas the original 25 class boiler had a calculated evaporation rate of 55,000lb/hr, an ihp of 3,200 gives a steam consumption of 17·2lb/ihp-hr which is in line with large American power having similar features. With No 3450 producing 4,492ihp at a steam rate of 66,000lb/hr, the consumption works out at 14·8lb/ihp-hr or little more than a British Railways Class 7 Britannia 4–6–2 at maximum evaporation, recorded as 14·4lb/ihp-hr at 35% cut-off and 105kph.

In 1982 the two Wardale experimental locomotives double-headed for a run on train 222, Alex Yard, Beaconsfield to Bloemfontein. On the outward run they climb towards Olienhoutplaas, with virtually smokeless combustion.

Climbing up to Kloofeind in 1983 The Red Devil *provides the power, while the Garratt (well winded) provides the smoke! No 3450 had by then the larger smoke deflectors (extended as far forward as clearances would allow), front fall plate removed, and the air supply for sanding provided by a compressor driven by a stoker engine.*

In terms of maximum evaporation again, E. S. Cox records a Britannia as producing 52ihp/sq ft of grate area, whereas the class 26 shows a figure of 64ihp/sq ft, with South African coal having about 12 per cent less calorific value than South Kirkby.

Given a new locomotive built to take full advantage of the detail features of No 3450, one might expect BR's Class 8P No 71000 to lose its position as the most efficient simple expansion locomotive ever built.

In traffic, No 3450 makes a superb express passenger locomotive, and *Continental Railway Journal* No 59 for Autumn 1984 details a magnificent run on the Orange Express, loaded to 20 vehicles, about 830 tonnes gross, against the normal load of 16 coaches, 670 tonnes. Despite two signal stops (one of nearly three minutes), two signal checks, and a permanent way slack, the locomotive knocked the 200 minutes running time down to 182.

As recorded, it is less happy in low-speed service, and on the return journey with about 1,060 tons, close to maximum load, the combined effects of defective sanding, and a rain squall just as the train was on a sharply-curved stretch of 1 in 80 caused slipping to a standstill. With wide open regulator and full forward gear, the locomotive simply had not sufficient tractive effort to re-start, and after much struggling the only recourse was to back down the line and try again, absence of further rain just enabling it to negotiate the sticky bit. Having got the train on the move, the locomotive's ability to develop high horsepower was used to belt along at 100kph to 110kph, easily recovering the half-hour lost by the stalling. The moral is that horsepower is ineffective without sufficient adhesion to absorb the force component at low speeds.

On another occasion No 3450 was double-headed with a GMAM Garratt on a heavy load from Beaconsfield to Bloemfontein. Possibly the theory was that the Garratt's superior adhesion and tractive effort would overcome the low-speed work, while No 3450's horsepower would roll the train once under way. However, the 'Red Devil's' features avoid the need for frequent stops to clean the fires from clinkery coal, and with a clear road ahead the driver ran right through De Brug station. When it came to the long steep climb to Kloofeind the Garratt was winded and running at about half-pressure, but luckily the day was dry and the pair made it to the summit, with No 3450 barking away with its ultra crisp exhaust, and doing at least two-thirds of the work. The Garratt eventually dropped two plugs while at Bloemfontein shed, and had to be towed back dead. Obviously, the GMAM should also have been Wardalised before trying such a combination!

SAR's motive power costing exercise, reviewed in Chapter 8, credited the class 26 with its lower fuel consumption, and made it the most economic alternative available. The author has extrapolated the review to include a hypothetical 2–10–4 of similar overall weight to Watson's proposed class 22, but updated with class 26 features, providing thereby a highly economical locomotive with nearly 50 per cent more adhesion than the class 26. Such a machine plus a matching Garratt with interchangeable mechanical details would handle SAR's traffic far more economically than the current electric and diesel mix, but such an extreme change in policy is more than the dogmatic Afrikaaners could stomach, so they will continue to use less economic motive power, and discontinue services in order to 'economise', thus commencing the downward spiral typified by British Railways' disastrous policy of self-destruction.

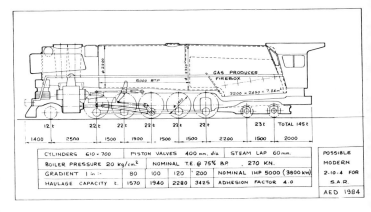

Author's 2–10–4 scheme, including Wardale features, for economic operation. See pages 202–3 for economic effectiveness.

Post Wardale

In 1984 No 3450 was involved in a collision with some runaway wagons, one of which wrapped itself round the front of the locomotive, causing extensive superficial damage. Some doubt was expressed as to whether the locomotive should be returned to service, but Beaconsfield shed got to work and repaired most of the damage, returning it to traffic

A post-Wardale development. No 3454 with transverse double Lempor exhaust to save extending the smokebox, speeds south from Grasplan in February 1985 with an 18-coach all stations train. Although up-grade, 1/500th-second exposure has not quite stopped it!   Christine Durrant

In 1985 form, with feedwater heater removed and fall plate restored, No 3450 makes a smoky exit from Orange River – the smoke having been organised by SAR's official photographer, possibly on a remit to 'prove' that modern steam is not smokeless! Nevertheless, the 19 coaches handled by No 3450 were shifted very much faster than 17 coaches dragged by two class 34 diesels on the previous Sunday!

in February 1985. The damaged feedwater heater was discarded as being too difficult to repair, and with it went the turbo feed pumps, always troublesome and supplanted by injectors. Exhaust from the turbo pumps provided most of the under-grate steam for clinker prevention, and the locomotive will now tend to be more clinker-prone. Certainly on a passenger run observed late in February 1985 the locomotive smoked heavily, whereas previously it was virtually smokeless.

Locomotive No 3454

Following the departure of Wardale, Beaconsfield has carried out a modification to class 25NC No 3454. A double Lempor exhaust system has been fitted, using identical nozzle clusters as on No 3450, but to save the cost of extending the smokebox the chimneys are arranged side-by-side. This locomotive was set to work in February 1985, and was observed at the end of that month working the same train as had been worked two days earlier by No 3450. The new conversion has a much harsher exhaust beat than the 'Red Devil' but according to driver and shed staff does in fact save both coal and water compared with a standard class 25NC, although the amount has not been quantified. Apart from the blastpipe and chimney, no other modifications have been incorporated, and the locomotive is noticeably more sure-footed than No 3450 which tends to slip every time it starts. After a while in service, No 3454 had smoke deflectors increased in height in rather a similar manner to No 3450, these being painted blue, while for a while the whole locomotive was in a very dark and barely discernible blue. Both Nos 3450 and 3454 seem now to have an artificially short life ahead of them.

CHAPTER 8
The Third Alternative

In any country having reasonably-priced supplies of indigenous energy it is commonsense both from the economic and strategic viewpoints to use such sources. The mining, cutting, pumping or other activity which produces such fuel also provides local employment, a particularly important factor in African countries which have severe unemployment problems. Furthermore, whatever happens politically, a country dependent on local fuel cannot be deprived by external interference. For a country like South Africa whose political practices rightly or wrongly invite such interference, it is the height of folly to subject a large and important part of the country's transport system to the vagaries of external political whim.

Prior to 1970, SAR had a very sensible policy of dependence on local coal-based energy, burned directly in steam locomotives on most routes, and used in power stations to generate electricity for such routes where traffic justified the heavy capital outlay. Diesel traction was limited to areas where the quantity and quality of water made steam traction difficult and expensive.

After 1970 this excellent policy was abandoned, and a diesel traction section was formed which seemed to be outside any sort of control by normal management channels—they were just fanatics! In 1970, before the first oil crisis, nine per cent of SAR's motive power fleet was dependent upon imported energy, an acceptable proportion for low-trafffic density lines with water problems and distant from coal sources. The world oil crises—highlighted for South Africa by political problems in Iran, which before deposition of the Shah was South Africa's main source of oil—had no effect upon the diesel fanatics. By 1980 twenty-seven per cent of the locomotive fleet was dependent upon imported oil and by 1984 this figure had increased to 34 per cent!

Apart from the strategic viewpoint, there is the cost involved. Oil is imported against USA dollars, and whereas in 1982 the South African Rand was worth $1·25, by the end of 1984 it was hovering around the 43 to 50 cent mark, meaning that despite minor reductions in the dollar oil price, the price in South African rands was about 2½ times that in 1982. In the case of spare parts for diesels, where the USA prices have been subject to inflation, the rand costs in South Africa have trebled in the same short period.

About 1980 it was realised that the costs of diesel traction were getting outrageous, so SAR's management set about a panic programme of electrification—the second alternative—based on the sound principle of retaining an indigenous energy base. In line with Afrikaaner political strategies cost was ignored, resulting in proposals and implementation of electrification on several routes where there is no hope of traffic demand rising to a level which will amortise the enormous capital cost of electrification. Put to a basic rule-of-thumb method, a general-purpose railway which does not carry sufficient traffic to warrant double track can never warrant electrification. During the 1980s period, when the World was entering and enduring a recession period, causing private industry to streamline and reduce staff, the South African government actually expanded its already enormous bureaucracy, debasing the currency and rocketing both inflation and interest rates! As a result of this, the break-even point for electrification, whose major financial input is capital, retreated.

What was never even considered was the third alternative, that is new and modern steam locomotives. To SAR management's limited outlook, steam traction meant the locomotives built 30 or more years ago, restricted in output by axle load restrictions no longer in force, and devoid of features now proved to be of great value. Accounting procedures basing figures on a 'per kilometre' value ensure that any locomotive in shunting service has a low kilometre denominator and therefore a 'high' cost. By shifting steam to shunting duties and keeping non-steam on line service, the figures have been cleverly fiddled to make steam seem grossly uneconomical. When a realistic cost investigation was belatedly carried out, steam was found to be the cheapest form of traction.

Meanwhile, a whole host of spurious reasons were invented and broadcast to indicate the unsuitability of steam traction, some of these, with suitable comment, being given below.

'Steam is uneconomic'

This opinion was reached by the time-honoured accountants' method of adding all the costs together and dividing by the number of locomotives to give a totally irrelevant average. It meant that brand-new diesels on main line work were being compared with 60-year-old steam locomotives on shunting duties, and voting the diesel the winner. When belatedly in 1982 a proper survey was carred out, it was found that 30-year-old steam locomotives were more economical than diesels of five to six years old, and that traffic would have to at least double before electrification became viable. New steam locomotives were not even considered. There has been no resultant policy change – on a railway which is losing money, the most economical form of motive power continues to be retired!

'Steam is heavy on maintenance'

Again, an accounting fiction. Costs are quoted 'per kilometre' with the result that any shunting locomotive running low kilometres has an equally low denominator to the cost equation. With steam largely relegated to shunting, an artificial 'high maintenance cost' is quoted for steam locomotives which in any case are much older than the diesels. It is interesting to note that by SAR's accounting methods a small shunting diesel costs double to maintain than a far larger main line diesel! Investigated figures show that a modern main line steam locomotive costs approximately as much as an equivalent diesel in maintenance.

'Steam cannot handle air-braked trains'

An incredible assertion in view of the fact that about three-quarters of the World's steam locomotives are air-braked! Several industrial users have fitted ex-SAR locomotives with air brakes, and these successfully handle SAR air-braked wagons. Of course, the assertion is aimed at the ignorant majority – politicians, public, and railwaymen who have never seen an air-braked steam locomotive – who believe what they are told because they have no means of questioning or disproving the assertion.

'Steam cannot haul the 20,000 ton trains we operate'

To start with, such trains form an infinitesimal proportion of the trains run by SAR, and are thus no excuse for a general retirement of steam. Secondly, while present-day SAR steam locomotives are insufficiently powerful for such loads, it is perfectly possible to construct those that are, and to use fewer locomotives per train than are required with electric or diesel traction.

'Steam cannot be run in multiple-unit'

Partially true inasmuch as no means of remotely controlling a steam locomotive boiler has been proven. However, remotely-driven steam locomotives were long a feature of push-pull passenger trains in Europe, and the same techniques can be used to run several steam locomotives, each with individual firemen, controlled by a single driver. The saving thus is in drivers who are paid more than

firemen. Development and perfection of equipment to replace the firemen undoubtedly would cost more than employing the firemen, especially in a country like South Africa with a large unemployment problem. Since running steam locomotives manned solely by firemen has been proven in European passenger service, there can be no question of safety problems.

'Multiple-unit diesels save crew costs'

This is of course true. What is never quoted officially is that energy costs for diesels are about four times crew costs for existing steam. The break-even point comes when on maximum gradient one uses eight or nine class 26 4–8–4s (each with driver and fireman) instead of six class 34 diesels with a single crew. With larger steam locomotives, such as the proposed 2–10–4, the lines actually diverge, in other words the more diesels one uses, the greater the margin by which extra oil cost exceeds the crew cost for steam. With Garratts, as would sensibly be used on such heavy service, the advantage for steam increases.

The above statements are quite radical and iconoclastic, apparently shattering the carefully nurtured myth that steam is uneconomic. How true are they? Are there any realistic figures to prove the case one way or the other? In view of the wholesale change-over from steam traction during the past 40 years, it is remarkable how little information is available on accurate and unbiased trials between one traction mode and the other. The reason is that such trials were rarely carried out – in a world obsessed with political revolution and the overthrow of colonialism no matter what the cost, one could add the overthrow of steam traction to be the *jihad* and hand round the hat for some sucker to pay the bill.

The first real evaluation was on the New York Central Railroad in the USA, where one of its latest 6,000hp Niagara class 4–8–4s was compared with a two-unit diesel of 4,000hp and a 6,000hp three-unit diesel. Based on an availability of 83 per cent for steam and 86.4 per cent for diesel, the comparative figures can be tabulated as below:

	Steam 6,000hp	Diesel 6,000hp	Diesel 4,000hp
Repairs	0.356	0.500	0.352
Fuel	0.410	0.420	0.280
Other	0.147	0.152	0.136
Total	0.913	1.072	0.768

Bearing in mind the above, it is very interesting to record that in January 1985 the Chesapeake & Ohio Railroad conducted a series of dynamometer car tests using 4–8–4 No 614 on coal traffic between Hinton and Huntington, West Virginia.

Railway	C&O	NYC	SAR	Ratio SAR/NYC
Gauge	4ft 8½in	4ft 8½in	3ft 6in	0.74
Locomotive class	J3A	S1b	26	–
Cylinders	27½in × 30in	25½in × 32in	24in × 28in	0.77†
Driving wheels	6ft 2in	6ft 7in	5ft 0in	0.76
Boiler pressure, lb/sq in	255	275	225	0.82
Tractive effort @ 85%	66,450	61,500	51,410	0.84
Grate area, sq ft	100	101	70	0.70
Heating surface, sq ft	4,821	4,819	3,104	0.64
Superheat, sq ft	2,058	2,073	788	0.38
Locomotive weight, tonnes	218.7	213.6	120*	0.56
Adhesion, tonnes	129.3	124.7	75*	0.60
Axle load, tonnes	32.5	31.2	19*	0.61
Maximum recorded ihp	–	6,600	4,475	0.68
Ihp/tonne, locomotive only	–	30.9	37.3	1.21

* Estimated weights, slightly higher than class 25NC
† Volume

These have been in connection with the proposed ACE 3000 high-efficiency steam proposal, and it is also possible that No 614 may be modified on similar lines to SAR's class 26. An announcement in *The Railway Gazette International* for January 1985 stated that the Chinese railways are also bringing out an improved locomotive based on class 26 technology, so it seems that Wardale on SAR has started something of which the World is taking notice.

C&O No 614 is of very similar dimensions and features to the NYC Niagara class compared above, and it is of interest to compare dimensions of these two American 4–8–4 with those of SAR's class 26.

Crew costs were irrelevant, as any combination carried the same crew. The message was that in higher speed service where horsepower counted more than tractive effort, 6,000hp of modern steam cost less than its equivalent in diesel. For low-speed operation the work could be done by 4,000hp diesels due to their total adhesion characteristics. Thus in a world which was speeding-up, diesels with high tractive effort/low-speed characteristics replaced steam whose characteristics were the opposite. The result — longer, heavier trains, at slower speeds and lesser frequencies, sending impatient shippers into the hands of road transport. Several USA railroads were thus dieselised into bankruptcy, and amazingly around the World railways anxious to emulate the soap opera fiction that the newest must be the best, followed suit with equally disastrous results. The best (or more accurately, the worst) example is British Railways.

Let us now recreate the table above, which is particularly relevant to South Africa. The NYC 'Niagara' 4–8–4 has been noted in international publications as being similar in appearance to the SAR class 25NC. This similarity is more than skin deep, for the two designs share such basics as cast steel beds, roller bearings throughout, and are coal fired by mechanical stokers. Dimensionally, through rail gauge, driving wheel diameter, and many other dimensions, the SAR locomotive is a miniatured version of the American to the ratio 3:4.

Let us now assume that the American locomotive has been improved in the same manner as SAR's class 26, which shows a 28 per cent fuel saving in identical freight service. Let us also assume that for some reason, the American locomotive's fuel consumption can only be improved by 15 per cent. Although the actual figure is far more, let us assume that for diesels, the fuel cost today is merely doubled. Now:

	Steam 6,000hp	Diesel 6,000hp	Diesel 4,000hp
Repairs	0.356	0.500	0.352
Fuel	0.349	0.840	0.560
Other	0.147	0.152	0.136
Total	0.852	1.492	1.048

The indications are very strongly that in the USA substantial savings may be obtained by a reversion to steam traction, when reasonably-priced coal is available. How does that compare with South Africa, the subject of this book? In 1982–3, following the conversion of class 25NC into the class 26 known as the 'Red Devil' due to its red livery an investigation was launched into the actual costs of steam and electric traction on the Kimberley to De Aar main line, and this was compared with a computer simulation of costs with electric traction. Wherever possible, the assumptions were biased in favour of diesel traction, as for example in allowing as many of the more powerful class 7E electrics as the inferior class 34 diesels in handling the traffic, and in exaggerating the times needed for coaling and watering steam at the terminals.

Loads per locomotive were limited by the available adhesion on ruling grades, and this determined the number of trains necessary to run the service, and therefrom the number of locomotives required. Four categories were included, class 7E, a Co-Co alternating current electric for which 19 locomotives were assumed. In fact, this number could be reduced to 13 although this would make little difference to the final result. The calculations were based on the

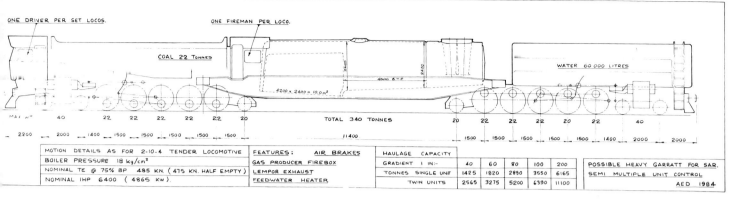

COAL 22 TONNES

WATER 60 000 LITRES

4200 x 2400 = 10.0 m²

MAIN WT 40 22 22 22 22 22 20   TOTAL 340 TONNES   20 22 22 22 20 22 40

MOTION DETAILS AS FOR 2-10-4 TENDER LOCOMOTIVE	FEATURES:	AIR BRAKES
BOILER PRESSURE 18 kg/cm²	GAS PRODUCER FIREBOX
NOMINAL TE @ 75% BP 485 KN. (475 KN. HALF EMPTY)	LEMPOR EXHAUST
NOMINAL IHP 6400 (4865 KW).	FEEDWATER HEATER

HAULAGE CAPACITY

GRADIENT 1 IN:-	40	60	80	100	200
TONNES SINGLE UNIT	1425	1820	2890	3550	6165
TWIN UNITS	2565	3275	5200	6390	11100

POSSIBLE HEAVY GARRATT FOR SAR. SEMI MULTIPLE UNIT CONTROL
AED 1984

Author's scheme for heavy duty Garratt with semi-multiple unit operation as described in text.

class 34 diesel, of Co-Co type, it being assumed that 19 would be needed and that several heavy trains already hauled by multiple diesels would remain so, only the currently steam trains being replaced by diesels. Similarly, the assumption is that even after electrification, the currently diesel trains will remain so hauled, although this is ridiculous.

Two categories of steam are included, class 25NC 4–8–4, of which 31 locomotives are calculated to be required, and class 26 rebuilt 4–8–4 which is allowed economies in fuel and water. Realistically, the class 26 should be allowed reduced running times due to its higher horsepower, and reduced terminal times due to less coal and water consumption, and reduced fire cleaning due to less clinker formation. The third alternative, that of new steam built to present-day weight limitations is ignored. This is particularly unfortunate as new steam in fact produces the lowest costs of all.

The number of locomotives to run the service was based on the haulage capacities of the various locomotive types over the ruling gradients of 1 in 80 northbound and 1 in 100 south-bound. The rated tractive effort of the various types, with those for steam calculated as 25% of adhesion weight, are tabulated below:-

To move the annual tonnage of 20 million, SAR's calculations mysteriously show that the locomotive requirements are for 19 diesels, the same number of electrics, or 31 4–8–4 steam locomotives. Here, clearly, electric traction is being penalised by restricting its southbound loadings, which are the limiting factor. The author's re-calculations using SAR's method show that the traffic could be handled by either 13 class 7E electrics, or 17 2–10–4 steam locomotives.

Cost of locomotives

For the capital cost calculations, SAR used R1,21 million for a class 7E and R0,702 for a class 34, these no doubt being current prices. For steam, the original cost of a 25NC was upgraded by inflation indices over the years to give R0,708 million for a 25NC, while R114,000 was added for the conversion cost of a class 26, capitalising it thus as R0,822 million. For the proposed new 2–10–4, the author has assumed the same cost per ton as a 25NC, plus ten per cent to cover design, jigs, and tooling. With an estimated locomotive and tender weight of 270 tonnes, this gives a cost per locomotive of R0,93 million. No conversion cost has been added for the Wardale features in the 2–10–4, since these will clearly have been designed into the engine.

Type	Class	Tractive effort kilonewtons/lb	Train loads (tonnes) North	South	Availability %
Electric	7E	320/72,000	1,705	1,705 (2,500)*	91
Diesel	34	218/49,050	1,332	1,705	87
Steam	25NC & 26	185/41,625	1,071	1,303	83
Steam	Proposed 2–10–4	270/60,635	1,570	1,705 (2,000)*	85

*Realistic tonnages.

Southbound train tonnages for electrics were restricted to those for diesels, which is unrealistic, the electrics being considerably more powerful. This is typical of the pro-diesel bias shown. For the table above, the author has similarly restricted the proposed 2–10–4 to the same tonnage, although pro rata to the 4–8–4 classes, and allowing for its higher power/weight ratio, it should be allowed about 2,000 tonnes, using the SAR calculation method.

Other cost assumptions for the proposed 2–10–4: :
Crew costs—pro rata to locomotive numbers, ie 17/31.
Energy costs—three percent less than for 26 class, due to reduced deadweight involved.
Maintenance costs—current steam costs reduced 17/31 for reduced number of locomotives and increased 270/223 pro rata to locomotive weight.
Shed costs—unchanged. *Water costs*—as for energy.

202

Comparative traction costs for various locomotive types between Kimberley and De Aar

Southbound approx 11·5 million tons/annum.
Northbound approx 8·5 million tons/annum.

Column	1	2	3	4	5	6
Traction	Electric	Electric	Diesel	Steam	Steam	Steam
Locomotive class	7E	7E	34	25NC	26	2–10–4
Southbound load, tonnes	1,705	2,500	1,705	1,303	1,303	2,000
Trains/year	6,763	4,606	6,763	8,836	8,836	5,757
Annual costs, R million.						
Electrification						
Interest and depreciation	2,897	2,897	–	–	–	–
Signals and Telegraph, interest and depreciation	4,948	4,948	–	–	–	–
Locomotives:						
Interest and depreciation	3,564	2,439	2,267	3,402	3,950	2,451
Crew costs	1,440	985	1,422	2,197	2,197	1,205
Energy costs	3,159	3,159	8,219	5,091	3,691	3,580
Locomotive maintenance	500	342	826	1,279	1,279	849
Catenery maintenance	280	280	–	–	–	–
Signal and Telegraph maintenance	711	711	–	–	–	–
Water costs	–	–	–	375	262	254
Shed costs	093	093	407	553	553	553
Total costs	17,592	15,854	13,141	12,897	11,932	8,892

Columns 1, 3, 4, & 5 are the figures as shown in the SAR report, and relate to late 1982. Column 2 is re-calculated to show the class 7E better utilised to run the traffic in fewer trains of maximum load for such locomotives. Column 6 shows the steam figures again re-calculated similarly for 2–10–4 locomotives of 22 tonnes axleload. Taking current steam working with class 25NC as a basic cost index of 100, the alternatives become:

Class 7E (SAR assumptions)	136
Class 7E (full loading)	123
Class 34	102
Class 26	93
New 2–10–4 proposal	69

Since these figures were prepared, the prime interest rate in South Africa has risen from 16–17 per cent to 24–25 per cent, particularly affecting electrification costs. Equally, mismanagement of the economy has led to a disastrous drop in the rand versus the US dollar, from R1.00 equals $1.25 to R1.00 equals 50 cents. This particularly affects diesel traction, not only the fuel but most of the spare parts having to be purchased in US dollars.

From the above, it is abundantly clear that even in late 1982, steam in any form was the most economic form of traction for South Africa, and SAR's report states: 'Steam is more economical than diesel traction for all traffic densities'. Electrification can be made economic, but not at present traffic levels. Indeed, compared to running trains with new high capacity steam locomotives, traffic would need to treble before electrification became viable.

The new steam locomotives included in the calculations are straightforward 2–10–4 general purpose machines presenting no real technical problems. The main working parts can be used under a Garratt capable of handling about 3,680 tonnes southbound, by the SAR method of calculation. Two of these, in semi-multiple-unit operation could handle 7,000 tonnes, or as much as four class 34 diesels in multiple.

'From where can we buy new steam locomotives?' is a commonly expressed question when one of the anti-steam brigade is eventually cornered. South African industry is well geared to produce steam locomotives, with two rolling stock manufacturers having erecting shops with overhead cranes of sufficient capacity for large steam power. There is no need today for a complete locomotive manufacturing works, with foundry, boiler shop, and all the other paraphernalia of the past. New steam locomotives can be assembled from sub-contracted components in just the same manner as diesels or electrics. Boilers much larger and more complex than the locomotive type are built in SA for power stations and similar installations. There is a wheel and axle specialist, a foundry with much expertise in rolling stock castings such as large bogie frames, to whom steam locomotive castings would present few problems. Any good wagon builder could supply the tenders, and the only imported components would need to be a few specialist items such as the larger roller bearings etc. All in all, new steam could be built in South Africa with a local content of 90 per cent to 95 per cent, compared with 50 per cent to 60 per cent for electrics or diesels.

South African steam is in twilight—an artificial twilight created by the shadow of those unable or unwilling to see that steam traction in a coal-producing country represents maximum economy of operation, and thus maximum profitability for the railway system.

Postscript

This book was written in 1985, and since it has some natural structure references 'today' generally refers to 1985, although all tabular details have been updated to the current year. During this interim, South African Railways were renamed South African Transport Services, but rolling stock continues to be delivered and outshopped lettered SAR. A very negative and bureaucratic management persisted until 1988 and there was talk of widespread branch line closure, similar to the worst excesses of Britain's Beeching regime a quarter of a century earlier. Fortunately, early 1988 saw the appointment of a new General Manager, Dr A. T. Moolman, whose general attitude has proved vastly more positive.

Main line steam almost ended in mid-1988, but a widespread outcry, especially from overseas enthusiasts caused a rethink, and a certain amount of steam traction is being retained from Kimberley to De Aar and Bloemfontein, until at least the early nineteen-nineties. Hopefully, this may even be continued for a little longer as it has been recognised that real steam working everyday freight traffic is a powerful attraction for steam enthusiasts worldwide. In September 1989 there is to be a steam festival centred on Kimberley during which a higher than normal proportion of freight traffic will be steam, plus some of the regular passenger trains. The success of such a programme will hopefully provide the incentive for similar programmes in later years, preferably in mid-winter when photographic opportunities are better.

Dr Moolman has now given the go-ahead for building the National Railway Museum at Krugersdorp, and this promises to be as good or better than any such institution anywhere in the world. The museum will house two rakes of useable passenger stock, numerous steam locomotives in working order, plus static exhibits. Furthermore, several extremely interesting steam locomotives are being restored to working order including classes 12A, 14CRB, GB, GL and GO, and possibly others in due course. Regional depots are being encouraged to retain a few steam locomotives for excursion service after cessation of regular steam services, and to date Bloemfontein, East London and Port Elizabeth have actively implemented this policy. At Kimberley, where steam remains in active service, there are several 'prestige' locomotives, including 16E 858, 26 3450, 25NC 3454 and 25 3511, which are maintained in good order. Given reasonable notice these will be run on requested freight trains for the benefit of steam enthusiasts, and overseas visitors should contact in advance of their visit:

The Regional Manager
P.O. Box Kimberley 620
South Africa

A narrow gauge museum has been set up at Humewood Road, Port Elizabeth, from which runs not only the weekly Apple Express, but also the shorter Dias Express, the latter along the beach front, using NGG16 class. The Patensie branch and some dock shunting will remain steam for the foreseeable future, using NG15 class, and steam freight along the narrow gauge main line may be encountered from time to time. Some of the older narrow gauge locomotives will be restored to working order, and an NGG11 is currently under overhaul at Bloemfontein works.

The Alfred County narrow gauge line, Port Shepstone to Harding, privatised as a commercial company, has proved to be a success with two or more freight trains running daily using NGG Garratts, plus a shorter distance tourist passenger train. Hopefully, this may be extended in principle to other lines.

As a postscript to Chapter 8, the annual report for 1987–88 revealed for the first time the cost of diesel fuel, with 1,541 diesels consuming 307 million rand of imported oil compared with 448 steam burning 18 million rand of indigenous coal per annum. As a raw average, this makes diesel fuel five times more expensive than steam per locomotive. The logical action to take will be to replace these diesels with modern, locally manufactured steam locomotives, but in railway management fashion unfortunately takes precedence over logic these days.

However, industrial users continue to acquire steam power, because of its economic advantages, and a book of this nature can never be totally up-to-date on such details. The most exciting current project, not yet finalised, is the proposed sale of between twenty and thirty 25NC 4–8–4s to Zimbabwe to replace uneconomic diesels and improve a critical motive power shortage.

Bibliography

The following works have been consulted, or can be recommended for further study of SAR steam locomotives.

Published books

Abbot R. A. S. *The Fairlie Locomotive*. David & Charles 1970.

Barrow Rev J. J. E. *Register of SAR Locomotives—* in preparation.

Binns D. *Kitson Meyer Articulated Locomotives.* Wyvern Publications 1987.

Cox E. S. *Locomotive Panorama*, Vol II. Ian Allan 1966.

Campbell E. D. *The Birth & Development of the Natal Railways.* Shuter and Shooter, 1951.

Carling D. R. *4–8–0 Tender Locomotives.* David & Charles 1971.

Durrant A. E. *The Mallet Locomotive.* David & Charles 1974.

Durrant A. E. *The Garratt Locomotive.* David & Charles 1969.

Durrant A. E. *Garratt Locomotives of the World.* David & Charles 1981.

Durrant A. E., Lewis C. P. and Jorgensen, A. A. *Steam on the Veld.* Ian Allan 1972.

Durrant A. E., Lewis C. P. and Jorgensen A. A. *Steam in Africa.* Struik 1981.

Holland D. F. *Locomotives of the South African Railways*, Vols I & II, David & Charles 1972.

Lewis C. P. and Jorgensen, A. A. *The Great Steam Trek.* Struik 1978.

Middleton J. N. and Jorgensen A. A. *Industrial Steam Locomotives of South Africa.* RSSA 1984.

Moir S. M. *Twenty Four Inches Apart.* Oakwood Press 1963.

Moir S. M. *Namib Narrow Gauge.* Oakwood Press 1982.

Paxton L. and Bourne D. *Locomotives of the South African Railways, A Concise Guide.* Struik 1985.

Rodgers D. C. *Steam in South Africa Today.* Ian Allan 1980.

Smith A. W. and Bourne D. E. *Spirit of Steam.* Struik 1983.

Talbot E. *Steam from Kenya to the Cape.* Continental Railway Circle 1975.

South African Railways. *Report of the General Manager*. Annually.

Diagram books

South African Railways.
Rhodesia Railways.
Caminhos de Ferro de Moçambique.

Periodicals

Beyer Peacock Quarterly Review.
Continental Railway Journal, London.
Henschel Review.
Locomotive Railway Carriage and Wagon Review.
Railway Gazette, London.
Developing Railways 1985, published by Railway Gazette International.
S A Rail, published by RSSA, Johannesburg & Durban.
South African Railways and Harbours Magazine, 1943–48, with serialised article 'The Locomotive in South Africa' by T. J. Espitalier and W. A. J. Day.

Papers

Class 25 Condensing Locomotives on the South African Railways, by Prof. Dr. Ing. R. Roosen. Proc Inst Locomotive Engineers 1960.

The Steam Locomotive, Motive Power for the Future, by D. Wardale. SAR Engineering Society, Pretoria, 1977.

Steam Locomotion, a reappraisal for an oil-starved World, by A. E. Durrant, Institution of Mechanical Engineers, Bulawayo, 1979.

Steam Locomotive Development in the 1980s, by A. E. Durrant, Society of Railway Engineers, Bulawayo, 1985.

S.A.R. internal publications

Locomotive Power Position. Monthly.
Classification of SAR Engines, Pretoria 1912.
Report of the Traction Policy sub-committee which determined the relative economies of the three available forms of motive power, 1983.

Acknowledgements

Rarely can a book of this magnitude be prepared single handed, even by an author resident in the country during the relevant main period, and this work is no exception. Apart from consultation with the books and papers mentioned in the bibliography, several individuals on SAR's staff have proved very helpful in providing information, drawings, old photographs, etc. for inclusion. In particular I would like to thank Mr P. A. Marais, Chief Mechanical Engineer who retired in 1985, and Messrs D. Wardale and P. A. Stow from his staff. Messrs E. Conradie and A. Clarke from the Library and Museum have been similarly helpful, together with Mr C. P. Lewis from the civil engineering department. Additionally, there are the numerous men from the motive power department, foremen, drivers, and firemen, without whose assistance some of the photographs would be lacking that little extra, and to these I extend heartfelt thanks.

Secondly, I thank those who have dug into their files and produced photographs, where mine have proved inadequate or non-existent.

Last, but far from least, I thank my wife, Christine, for her forbearance in the rôle of being a 'Steam widow'. As the photographic credits show, she is often out with me taking photographs, and is also very welcome sharing in the darkroom chores. At other times, when I am out alone, or ensconced in the study and library, she assumes the steam widow rôle only to produce, at the end of the day, a delicious meal! Truly, without Christine, life would be more difficult and less of a pleasure.

Stop Press · Stop Press · Stop Press · Stop Press · Stop Press · Stop Press ·

Swaziland Railways have purchased nine class 15AR from SAR – numbers 1571, 1788/92/95, 1827, 1967/68 and 2022/98 – these being the first locomotives actually owned by SR. In addition, 1856 has been bought as a hulk for spare parts (see Chapter 4 and pages 83–4).

For details of the GMAM class see pages 115, 140, 150 and 152. The sale of 4090 and 4129 to Australia has now fallen through, due to lack of funds. On the other hand, Enyati Railway is buying 4083 and 4088. Tweefontein Colliery are buying 4105/13/48 via Dunn's, due to an expected traffic increase.

Loraine Gold Mine has tendered for two 19D, 2734 and 3369 (see pages 103–4 and 156).

South African Transport Services have issued an extensive press release on locomotive preservation, too long for inclusion in this book, but whose details will doubtless be published in *SA Rail* and *Continental Railway Journal* (see Bibliography).

Index